P9-DDI-209

Defining moments

How God Shapes Our
Character Through CRISIS

RICK
EZELL

InterVarsity Press
Downers Grove, Illinois

InterVarsity Press
P.O. Box 1400, Downers Grove, IL 60515-1426
World Wide Web: www.ivpress.com
E-mail: mail@ivpress.com

InterVarsity Press® is the book-publishing division of InterVarsity Christian Fellowship/USA®, a student movement active on campus at hundreds of universities, colleges and schools of nursing in the United States of America, and a member movement of the International Fellowship of Evangelical Students. For information about local and regional activities, write Public Relations Dept., InterVarsity Christian Fellowship/USA, 6400 Schroeder Rd., P.O. Box 7895, Madison, WI 53707-7895.

Cover illustration: Terje Rakke/ Image Bank

ISBN 0-8308-2327-1

Printed in the United States of America ∞

Library of Congress Cataloging-in-Publication Data

Ezell, Rick, 1956-
    Defining moments: how God shapes our character through crisis / Rick Ezell.
      p. cm.
    ISBN 0-8308-2327-1 (pbk.: alk. paper)
    1. Suffering—Religious aspects—Christianity.   I. Title.

BV4909 .E89 2001
248.8'6—dc21

2001024033

22 21 20 19 18 17 16 15 14 13 12 11 10 9 8 7 6 5 4 3 2 1

19 18 17 16 15 14 13 12 11 10 09 08 07 06 05 04 03 02 01

To my brothers and sisters—
Ann,
Linda,
Jerry and
Micky—
who have helped to define my life.

Acknowledgments

I am grateful for the support and encouragement I have received from InterVarsity Press during the development of this book. This book filtered through many people at IVP before its completion, and I am thankful for the expertise and care each has given. Two of those people stand out: my dear friend Jim Connon, for encouraging my writing, and Cindy Bunch, who has been a joy to work with as editor throughout the project.

I am indebted to Carol Hendrickson for her labor over the manuscript proofreading, editing and offering suggestions.

I want to thank the members of Naperville Baptist Church for their encouragement and support of me as their pastor.

I am fortunate to have John Claiborne, Lee Messersmith and Lloyd Hendrickson to work alongside of me as a team who seek to help people say yes to Jesus. I am thankful to Jan Porter and Pat Hill, who handle many of my administrative tasks.

I can't begin to thank God for my wife, Cindy, and our daughter, Bailey. They have touched my life and marked my life far beyond words. Thanks.

Contents

Introduction

Where the English language would use the single word *crisis*, the Chinese language uses not one but two characters to form the word. The first character means danger; the second means opportunity. In other words, in the Chinese way of writing, the outcome of a crisis situation—either positive or negative—depends on the individual's response. Thus a crisis becomes a turning point.

Into every life come events that can make or break a person. These events can be wedges that drive us further from God or they can be magnets that draw us closer to him. Within the dark cloud of tragedy and misfortune lies the silver lining of God's grace. In order for us to experience that grace we need to understand how God works in distressing situations to define our lives.

Throughout the Bible we find story after story of how God worked through the crises of someone's life in order to shape that person's character. These stories are much like our stories; only the names and the places are different. The calamity and misfortune recorded in the scriptural stories must have felt very much the same as our own. Consequently we can learn from the biblical characters' responses to their crises.

In the pages that follow you will read about a prophet who ran away from God but ended up running into God; a father of a nation who needed to change before he could see God; a distressed woman who thought her world had fallen apart, only to discover the hope and power of new life three days later; three teenagers who found themselves having to make a choice that meant life or death; a crippled man who thought his fifteen minutes of fame would lead to his demise, only to be granted the wealth of a king; and others. In these compelling stories we will experience grace, witness miracles, foster hope and encounter help. The tender hand of God will become evident to you throughout the experience.

As we examine the defining moments of the biblical characters, a fresh perspective on our personal trials begins to take form. Taking a cue from our biblical counterparts, we are enriched and defined by the tragedies and misfortunes and everyday obstacles of human existence—if we allow God to work through our situations. No one likes painful events and no one prays for personal crises, but when they blow through our lives, God can use them to instruct us. They can be instruments that compel us to look at God afresh, to see his countenance and his favor upon our lives. Touched by the loving hand of God, our calamities can fashion us more nearly into the likeness of God's Son.

Perhaps you find yourself in the cross hairs of a crisis. Are the tears of disappointment filling your eyes? Is your integrity being put to the test? Are you being treated unfairly? Is your health giving way? Are you up against an overwhelming obstacle? Are you crippled emotionally or physically? Are your expectations not being met? Don't give up. You may be one step away from a miracle and one heartbeat away from grace. Your response to your crisis may spell the difference between danger and opportunity.

My hope and prayer is that you will discover in your crisis your defining moment.

One

When You Are Running from God

I n the middle of the night a freight train speeds effortlessly along. As the locomotive rounds a turn, a bus transporting convicted criminals straddles the tracks. In one mad, climactic moment the train slams into the bus, pushing it a hundred yards down the steel tracks and causing sparks to fly before the wreckage bursts into flames.

Could there be any survivors?

Authorities arrive to find a dazed prison guard. Minutes later ankle and wrist irons are found—open. The federal marshal holds up the irons and announces, "We have a fugitive."

Thus begins the silver-screen remake of the 1960s television series *The Fugitive*. The suspenseful movie is about Chicago surgeon Richard Kimball, who is falsely accused and convicted of his wife's murder. As the movie unfolds, Dr. Kimball keeps one step ahead of the authorities as he lives his life on the run.

Jonah, too, was a fugitive. An escapee. A man on the run. As a Hebrew prophet, Jonah's orders came from on high. He had been obedient before when instructions had come. But now . . . well, things were different now. This time he had been instructed to preach in Nineveh, capital of the

Assyrian Empire. Nineveh was the epitome of everything Jonah hated in the Gentile world; it stood for godless tyranny. Nothing was more repugnant to Jonah than the idea of traveling there to preach repentance.

Let's focus our mind's eye on the people we find it most difficult to love. On the screen of our conscience may flash the faces of people with a different color of skin, with a different culture or from a different socioeconomic class. Or we may see people not unlike us in appearance and status, yet for some reason we despise them. Now let's consider that we have been given a directive from God to go to those individuals and offer our help, our love and our goodness.

That would be difficult for me to do. But that's just the situation Jonah wrestled with. He had heard from God. He had also heard from his fear and his prejudices and his pride. And when God said, "Go," Jonah said, "No."

Jonah ran.

He's not unlike us. We, too, run. We, too, are fugitives. We run from the haunts of our past, from the horrors of our fears, from the heaviness of our responsibilities and even from the help of our God. As the hymn writer Robert Robinson observed:

> Prone to wander, Lord, I feel it;
> Prone to leave the God I love.[1]

Eventually we'll learn, as Jonah did, that you can run but you cannot hide.

Running away from God, Jonah was caught in a storm at sea that threatened the life of everyone on board the ship bound for Tarshish. The sailors threw him into the angry waves. Treading water and hoping for a miracle, Jonah lost strength and was about to give up hope. I'm sure he thought, *It can't get any worse than this.* But it could. And it did. Jonah was in for the ride of his life.

Listen to this recollection of Jonah's situation: "The currents swirled about me; all your waves and breakers swept over me. . . . 'I have been banished from your sight. . . .' The engulfing waters threatened me, the deep surrounded me. . . . I sank down. . . . My life was ebbing away" (Jonah 2:3-7). He was sinking deep into the water, on the verge of drowning.

Then came a huge fish with its mouth opening up to swallow him. Suddenly Jonah was not drowning in the ocean any longer but sloshing about inside a fish's belly.

If you use your imagination to recreate the scene inside the fish, it will terrify you. In the darkness gastric juices washed over Jonah, burning his skin, eyes, throat and nostrils. Oxygen was scarce and each frantic gulp of air was saturated with saltwater. The rancid smell of partially digested food caused Jonah to throw up repeatedly until nothing remained in his stomach. Everything he touched had the slimy feel of the fish's stomach lining. He felt claustrophobic. With every turn and dive of the great fish, he slipped and skidded in the cesspool of digestive fluids. There were no footholds or handles to hold on to, no blankets to keep him warm from the cold in the depths of the sea.

I apologize if you were planning to go to Red Lobster for lunch. But this graphic portrayal of Jonah in the fish's stomach is not an attempt to nauseate you. The physical surroundings, I believe, reflected Jonah's spiritual condition at this point. Spiritually he was as distant from God as was the fish from dry land. Spiritually he was as dirty from disobedience to God as was the vileness of the fish's stomach.

Today we gloss over sin, spruce it up, gift-wrap it and make it look pretty. We cover it up with less evil-sounding words like *affair, fraud, embezzlement* or *misdemeanor*. But in God's eyes sin is still as vile as rancid smells, partially digested food and vomit.

Jonah had disgraced his calling as a prophet. A disobedient prophet, a fallen evangelist, a backslidden Christian—they all share the common denominator of shame. They were given a task, but they disobeyed. They took matters into their own hands. They chose to live out their lives on their terms instead of God's. Jonah was not alone. Abraham, Moses, David, Peter—in fact, virtually all of the Bible's notables, excluding Jesus—could fall into this category.

> In God's eyes sin is still as vile as rancid smells, partially digested food and vomit.

Whenever we begin looking away from God, walking down the path of our own choosing, we are heading toward destruction. How do we avoid taking matters into our own hands? A good place to start would be doing the opposite of what Jonah did. That is, we should start listening to God, being sensitive to his plan and obeying his word.

I would like to say that I have always been sensitive to God's plan and obedient to his calling, but I haven't. I'm a lot like Jonah. I, too, have been given a task and have run away from that task. I, too, have taken matters into my own hands. I, too, have chosen to pursue my vocation on my terms instead of God's.

I never wanted to be a pastor, though that's what God called me to be. For years I was a youth minister and thoroughly enjoyed working with students and their parents. An excitement and vitality existed within youth ministry that I had not seen in pastoral ministry. While I loved to preach, and while many people had affirmed my gifts in that area, I was reluctant to respond to God's call to pastoral ministry. And why should I? My ministry with students had always been effective. Teenagers were coming to Christ, many were being called to ministry, and others were becoming effective leaders in their college ministries.

While I refused to obey God's call, I went through a period of depression. I was in ministry, but I was not in the center of God's will. I was running from God's desire because I felt comfortable and secure with my current status. I wanted to stay where I was.

God had different ideas.

Like Jonah, I felt discouraged and despondent at times. I was distant from God. A hunger for God and his Word was not present within me. As effective as my ministry was, it was not fulfilling me. These were not pleasant times, but as I look back upon them, I realize they were profitable times. A football coach told his team after a disheartening loss, "We learn almost nothing in victory, but we learn much in defeat." Belly-of-the-fish experiences are not enjoyable places, but they can be teachable locations.

If we are thinking about running from God, Jonah's story has some important lessons to teach us. They are lessons that anyone on the run *will* learn, but we can learn them before we take off, trying to get beyond the long arm of God's laws. Or we can learn them as we venture out into uncharted waters where storms and creatures of pain and misery lie in wait for castaways.

What are those lessons? Let us sit back in our chair to watch on the big screen as the lessons of life unfold in one of the world's first docudramas— the story of a man named Jonah, a fugitive.

Who Do We Blame?

Jonah's painful ride was caused by his own rebellion. Jonah learned this important lesson as he was stuffed into the fish's stomach. He stated, "In *my* distress I called to the LORD" (Jonah 2:2, emphasis added).

Often when we find ourselves in painful predicaments, we want to play the blame game. We want to blame our past, our parents, our partners or our place in life. We point a finger at someone else. But often we have no one to blame but ourselves.

In the belly of the fish Jonah realized that he had no one to blame but himself. He had inflicted his predicament on himself by his selfish defiance.

Are We Fast Enough to Outrun God?

Running from the Lord is like trying to draw a round square—it presents a logical impossibility. God is omnipresent, and we can't escape from someone who is everywhere.

The psalmist asked the question "Where can I flee from [God's] presence?" And then he answered:

> If I go up to the heavens, you are there;
>   if I make my bed in the depths, you are there.
> If I rise on the wings of the dawn,
>   if I settle on the far side of the sea,
> even there your hand will guide me,
>   your right hand will hold me fast. (Psalm 139:7-10)

If we drift on a raft in the middle of the ocean, God is there. If we camp in a cave in the mountains, God is there. If we reside in a mansion in suburbia, God is there. If we live in a cardboard shelter underneath an overpass, God is there. If we are adrift in a sea of immorality, God is there. If we remain distant, with a heart that is cold and hidden, God is there.

God is everywhere. We cannot run to any place where he is not. When we run from him, we end up bumping into him. There is nowhere to run, nowhere to hide. No matter where we go, we run into God.

Jonah forgot something when he thought he had outdistanced God. We can't run from God without running through him and winding up running toward him. Jonah bet on the false idea that he could flee from the presence of God. He lost.

Rebellion Has a Ripple Effect on Others

Disobedience toward God often has a negative effect, bringing a storm that can shipwreck those around us. Whether we realize it or not, the consequences of our actions have an effect on others. Always.

Lying, embezzling, speeding, cheating, financial misdealing, alcoholism and child abuse have a ripple effect on all those in their wake. Inappropriate behaviors affect us and those around us. John Donne was right when he recorded, "No man is an Island, entire of it self; every man is a piece of the Continent, a part of the main."[2]

Jonah learned this lesson the hard way. God commanded that he go to Nineveh, but Jonah had other plans. "He went down to Joppa, where he found a ship bound for that port. After paying the fare, he went aboard and sailed for Tarshish to flee from the LORD" (Jonah 1:3). Tony Evans, writing in *Our God Is Awesome*, says, "Note that Jonah 'paid the fare' himself because he was trying to run from God. Whenever you run *with* God, he pays the fare. When you try to run *from* God, you always pay."[3]

Jonah ultimately paid in the form of a storm that inflicted its wrath on him and all who were around him. He may have thought, *It's my decision. My disobedience and rebellion will not affect anyone else.* But try to explain that to the sailors caught in the storm. Their problems—the storm blasts in their faces—had been created by someone else. They were fearful for their lives because of a rebellious prophet. Jonah eventually divulged, "I know that it is my fault that this great storm has come upon you" (Jonah 1:12).

The Storm That Chased Him Home

The storms God sends are not meant to sweep us away but to bring us home. If we don't understand this critical lesson, the suffering and hardship we endure during the storms of our lives make no sense. When tragedy strikes, we may automatically assume that God is punishing us. Nothing could be farther from the truth. While God does chastise us when we disobey, the storms are not meant to punish us but to point us toward home and help.

The Bible describes another fugitive. Choosing to leave his family's home and his father's help, he ran to a distant land. He squandered all his money and ended up living as a slave feeding pigs. This lifestyle wasn't the bottom of the barrel of existence; it was looking up at the bottom. But in the midst of this "storm" the prodigal came to his senses. And because of the mire and the muck and the slop and the stench, he ventured home for help (Luke 15:11-24).

Often we have to weather a storm that takes everything from us before we can see the way home. That is the way with prodigal people and fugitives. Like Jonah, we choose not to go back to God until we have endured a storm and lost everything.

If we live as fugitives, on the run from God, the Good Shepherd will lead us back home the moment we give up trying to save ourselves and are willing to let him save us his own way.

Giving Up

Sometimes we have to experience the feeling of death before we can know the freedom of life. In a spiritual sense we have to give up before we can be raised up. When we realize there's nothing more we can do, then God can intervene and save us.

When Jonah gave up the hope of surviving, God intervened and saved him.

> To the roots of the mountains I sank down;
> the earth beneath barred me in forever.
> But you brought my life up from the pit,
> O LORD my God. (Jonah 2:6)

Jonah had to die to his own desires before he could live.

In the highlands of Scotland sheep often wander off into the rocks and get into places they can't get out of. The grass on these mountains tastes sweet, and the sheep like it. They will jump down ten or twelve feet to a ledge with a patch of grass, and then they can't jump back up again. The shepherd hears them bleating in distress. The shepherd may leave them there for days, until they have eaten all the grass and are so weak that they cannot stand. Only then will the shepherd put a rope around the sheep and pull them up out of the jaws of death.

Why doesn't the shepherd attempt a rescue when the sheep first get into the predicament? The sheep are so foolish and so focused on eating that they would dash away from the shepherd, go over the precipice and destroy themselves.

Such was the case with Jonah. And such is the case with us. Sometimes we need to experience a little bit of death before we can enjoy the abun-

> Sometimes we need to experience a little bit of death before we can enjoy the abundance of life.

dance of life. The Lord will rescue us the moment we have given up trying, realizing that we can't liberate ourselves, and cry to him for help.

And at that moment God does something miraculous. He offers a gift—a gift of grace and mercy. Just like salvation came to Jonah, rescue will come to us.

When God reaches down through the storm into the murky waters to save us, it is an act of grace.

The Gift of Grace

If the movie of Jonah's life stopped here, we would think that God was a rather jealous and vindictive being. Thus far in this story we have witnessed a great city, a great wind and a great fish, but the background of this picture is scattered with reminders of God's great grace. Because of God's grace, the underlying lesson is this: God often breaks us in order to remake us.

For almost anything good to be made, it first must be broken. A tree is broken and a house is built. Soil is broken and a crop is grown. Grain is broken and bread is baked. People are broken and caring, compassionate believers are reborn. Often it is out of our brokenness that our greatest influence comes. Often before God uses a man or woman greatly he first breaks them severely.

A church ordered new stained glass windows for its sanctuary. All the windows arrived except for the largest panel for the front of the church. The congregation anxiously waited this final panel's delivery. When the large piece arrived, they found the glass had been broken in transit. The people were dismayed. But then a skilled artist in the church asked if he could take the pieces and try to make a suitable replacement window. In a short while the artist unveiled the window he had fashioned. The entire congregation felt that the artist's masterpiece was more beautiful than the original. What was broken was remade into something spectacular.

God broke Jonah to remake him.

When the prophet was overboard and overwhelmed, "the LORD provided a great fish to swallow Jonah, and Jonah was inside the fish three days and three nights" (Jonah 1:17). For three days and three nights Jonah endured in the harsh womb of God's grace. Yes, grace. God did provide this great fish to swallow Jonah; he could have let him drown. Then God provided the great fish to vomit Jonah onto dry land. That, too, was grace.

God's grace sometimes comes in ways we would never expect.

Grace changed Jonah's life. This touch from God's hand was the defining moment of Jonah's life. Before this experience, several adjectives could have been employed to describe Jonah: *stiff-necked, resistant, stubborn, hardhearted, rebellious*. After this experience, other words could be used to describe this changed man: *broken, cleansed, contrite, new, obedient*. Grace has that effect on people.

Grace is the glue that takes the pieces of our broken lives and binds them into something new and beautiful. Grace is the welcome mat that says to the repentant prodigal, "Welcome home." Grace is the sponge that cleans the blotched record of our sins so that they are remembered no more. Grace is the rescuer that waits till we have depleted our energy to gently wrap an arm around our exhausted bodies and carry us to shore. Grace is the calling that God grants to a once-wayward prophet, energizing him for effective service. Grace is the announcement that there is life after failure and there is hope for broken, rebellious people.

I experienced that grace when I finally said yes to God's call upon my life. It made all the difference in the world.

Jonah learned what we need to learn about God's grace. As one hymn writer relates, "Mercy there was great, and grace was free."⁴ Jonah discovered God's unbelievable mercy and unmeritable grace. They were free.

The gift of grace to a rebellious and disobedient person is a future after failure and a hope after rebellion. That is the surprise of the cross and the empty tomb. That is the surprise of God to Jonah—and to every rebellious child.

Will We Open the Gift?

One of the many tragedies of life is that God's grace—his free gift of unmerited favor and love—is too often left as an unopened package. Given but not accepted. Presented but not opened.

In the story of Jonah the one verse that stands out most to me is this:

Those who cling to worthless idols
forfeit the grace that could be theirs. (Jonah 2:8)

If the bleating sheep runs from the shepherd, it will have forfeited his pull to freedom. And if Jonah had chosen not to receive God's free gift of grace, he would have forfeited his hope of salvation, his chance for reinstatement and his opportunity to become reusable and reclaimed for God's work.

The conclusion of the movie *The Fugitive* has uncanny parallels with Jonah's life. As Dr. Kimball continues to run from the police and the federal marshal, he learns the identity of his wife's real killer. He also discovers that his friend, a fellow doctor, set up the killing. Now his wife's killer is trying to kill him. And all the while the federal marshal who has been tracking Dr. Kimball since the train wreck is closing in on him. In one gut-wrenching move after another Dr. Kimball eludes each of his potential killers. Finally the federal marshal arrests him.

In catching Dr. Kimball the marshal frees him. Why? Unknown to the killer, to the doctor who had set up the killing and to the Chicago police, the federal marshal had uncovered the truth that Dr. Kimball was innocent. After Dr. Kimball slides into the back seat of the federal marshal's car, the marshal takes off Dr. Kimball's handcuffs. Since at the outset of the chase the marshal had said that he didn't care if Kimball were innocent or guilty, Dr. Kimball now says to the marshal, "I thought you didn't care."

The marshal replies with a chuckle, "Don't tell anybody."

When one reads Jonah's story, it appears that God didn't care. With the storm threatening Jonah and the large fish swallowing him, it even appears that God was trying to kill Jonah. But he was not. God cared (and, unlike the federal marshal in *The Fugitive*, he wanted all to know it). He was trying to save Jonah. He didn't want him to live as a fugitive but as a free man.

When we stop our running and accept the grace that God offers, we too will live in freedom and fulfillment.

Study Questions

1. Think about a time in your life when you were disobedient to God. How did you feel?

2. Who is the person in your life who is most difficult for you to love?

3. How would you describe your relationship with God at the lowest point in your life?

4. Have you been given a task by God and then run away from that task?

5. How does your level of satisfaction with your life affect your response to God's call?

6. What have you learned when you were disobedient?

7. What price have you paid when you have run from God?

8. What does the statement "We have to give up before we can be raised up" mean to you?

9. Describe a time when the grace of God brought refreshment and redirection to your life.

10. Read Jonah 2:8: "Those who cling to worthless idols forfeit the grace that could be theirs." How do those who cling to worthless idols forfeit grace?

Two

When You Need
to Change

*T*hree months before my daughter was born I made a statement at a party that I soon wished I could take back. In front of twenty-five friends (most of whom had reared children) I calmly remarked, "Having this baby will not change my life." Momentary silence was followed by an eruption of deep belly laughter. A few people even began rolling on the floor. The smirks and giggles and hounding went on for what seemed an eternity. I wanted to crawl under the sofa.

Three months later I discovered the reasons for the laughter. This wonderful and beautiful child, whom I had had a part in conceiving, cried, experienced fits of rage and lacked proper etiquette. Because of her entrance into my world, I rarely slept through the night or slept in on Saturdays. Watching a ball game or my favorite television show uninterrupted became an impossibility. Discretionary money for golf games and dates with my wife almost disappeared. Going to the mall on a moment's notice? Out of the question.

I had to eat my words again and again. Having a baby *does* change one's life.

The reality is, being *alive* changes one's life. The only constant in this world is change. "Everything flows and nothing stays," proclaimed Heraclitus, the ancient Greek philosopher. "You can't step twice in the same river."[1] To be alive, whether parenting a baby or not, means perpetual change.

A Change Reaction
While some people thrive on change, it is frightening to many of us, generating stress. Sometimes it seems that no one but a wet baby likes change. How do we often react to it?

We resist. If we are honest with ourselves, we hate and love change all at the same time. We have a neurotic tendency for wanting life to get better while desiring it to stay the same. We all resist change at some level and on some issues.

We recoil. Like the animal whose nostrils flare and muscles tighten at a sudden sound or movement, our primal nerves tense in the face of sudden change. Our first instinct is not to say, "Good, we're going to have constructive change." Our first reaction is often to panic and run.

We fear. Innovations, improvements and intrusions in our world often alarm and concern us, if not downright scare us. Yet it's not really the prospect of change we fear (consider, for example, our love of variety and newness); rather, we are afraid of the unknown.

We resent. The threat of change implies the giving up of certain rights or privileges, or at least a rousing from comfortable ruts and routines. We resent the inconvenience and frustration brought on by changes. Or we resent the traditions and heritage of our past being sacrificed for the modern.

Change need not be our enemy, although we often respond as if it is. In fact change may be the best thing that ever happened to us. It can help us see God.

A Man in Need of a Change
Jacob was born a twin, the second baby out of the womb. Upon entering this world, Jacob was clutching the heel of his brother, Esau. From that moment on, he was forever clutching what was rightfully his brother's. He

eventually cheated Esau out of his birthright and then his blessing.

If Jacob were alive today, many corporations would be delighted to employ him. A born competitor, he was determined to win. No matter the cost or the deception. He knew how to ascend the ladder of success. He was in control. No one could stop him from being on the top.

But the main event of Jacob's life changed all of that. It was a wrestling match. It was not Greco-Roman or Olympic freestyle or sumo or WWF. This was a wrestling match with . . . well, we will discover his opponent in just a moment.

The consummate competitor met his stiffest competition in the middle of the night. This sparring match was full of surprises. This experience shows how God can take a con artist and change him into a man of integrity. God redirected Jacob, bent on climbing his own hill of accomplishment, to moving toward a God-purposed life. His will was broken while his spirit was kept intact. God converted a cheater into a person of character. Jacob (whose name meant "he deceives") was given a new name, Israel ("he struggles with God"). This defining moment determined his destiny.

God Uses Crises to Get Our Attention

Not all crises that occur in our lives come from God, but God can take the frustrating experiences that are beyond our control and teach us a lesson. He can take the rough roads we travel and paint road signs along them that will instruct us and change us for the better. As long as we are content with the status quo, little change will occur. But once we are dissatisfied enough, we are motivated to allow God to perform some renovation work in the interior of our lives.

Such was Jacob. He had not seen his brother, Esau, for twenty years. Then Esau sent word that he was coming to see Jacob with four hundred men at his side. Jacob was fearful.

Was he thinking that Esau would treat him like he had treated Esau earlier in life? Plenty of time had elapsed for Esau to stir the boiling pot of revenge. Jacob was in trouble. He had no more tricks up his sleeve. He finally was forced to face up to his past. To Jacob's credit, he did not run away from the crisis.

He divided his people into two groups and marched them away in opposite directions (see Genesis 32:7-8). In case Esau attacked one group, the other one would be spared. "That night Jacob got up and took his two wives, his two maidservants and his eleven sons and crossed the ford of the Jabbok. After he had sent them across the stream, he sent over all his possessions. So Jacob was left alone" (Genesis 32:22-24). Jacob was fearful and felt threatened. He worried for his life.

Jacob was in a crisis and God was seeking Jacob's undivided attention.

When I was a teenager, I visited the youth leader of my church in the hospital. I walked into the room and asked, "Gary, why are you here?" Before he could answer, his wife replied, "Gary is so busy and on the go so much that the only way God could get his attention was to put him in a hospital bed."

In my naiveté I asked, "Well, Gary, does God have your attention?"

A wry smile came on Gary's face. "He sure does. Never have I been so open to hear from God."

God can use the crises of our lives—be they sickness, accidents, job loss, divorce or whatever—to get our attention. At few other times can God get through to us with such crystal clarity. In those moments we can change our focus as well as our direction.

Several years ago three dedicated Christian businessmen in my church lost their jobs. After several weeks of job searching, they came to me individually to talk. Interestingly, each wanted to know what I thought about him leaving the business sector and enrolling in seminary to pursue a ministerial vocation. One common thread ran through each man's story. Each prefaced his remarks by saying, "You know, I've been doing a lot of serious thinking lately."

These were fine Christian laymen. Eventually they found jobs and none enrolled in seminary. But by their own admission, their ears had previously been closed to God's voice. It took the loss of a job to jar them out of complacency.

Here's the point: God uses the crises of life, those near-tragic events in our lives, to jar us, to wake us, to get our attention. In our uncomfortable experiences he desires to get through to us. He wants to teach us some lessons.

We must never forget that God comes into our lives not only to comfort our affliction but also to arouse us from a state of complacency. These encounters with God, while they are uncomfortable, are teachable moments. Provided, that is, we allow God to speak and have his way with us.

Whatever the crisis, God can use it to rivet our attention on him. He wants to speak to us. His words may be uncomfortable, but they will be useful.

Our Greatest Fights Are Often with God, Not the Devil

The story of Jacob surprises us with another twist. God is the intruder in our lives. He sometimes invades our lives not to bring comfort but to wage a war. As strange as it may sound, there are times when we fight with God. Please understand that I'm not implying that we don't have fights with the devil or that spiritual warfare does not occur. Temptation is real. But often it is easier to say no to the devil than it is to say yes to God.

> Often it is easier to say no to the devil than it is to say yes to God.

Just ask Jacob.

As Jacob was alone that night, waiting for the arrival of his brother, a most unusual thing happened. "A man wrestled with him till daybreak" (Genesis 32:24). Thinking he was all by himself on a riverbank, Jacob was surprised by an aggressor. How was he accosted? From the front? Hardly. If it were a frontal assault, I think, Jacob would have reasoned with him. "Listen, friend, we can work out this disagreement. Let's have a drink and discuss the situation. We don't need to fight."

I believe the attacker surprised him from the rear, throwing his arms around him so Jacob was forced to retaliate. Who was Jacob's attacker? Was it Esau? Taking a page out of Jacob's book, Esau could have schemed and deceived his brother with a surprise strategy. Good guess. But no. Maybe it was one of Esau's men—a thug who happened along and saw an opportunity to mug a loner. Possibly. But again, no.

Jacob's attacker was none other than God himself.

Alone at night, Jacob wrestled with God. And of all the fights that Jacob had experienced in his life, of scheming and climbing and success, his most difficult fight was with the Almighty.

Just ask Jesus.

Jesus' toughest fight was not in the desert as the devil tempted him with pleasure, power and prestige. His most difficult battle was in the garden called Gethsemane (a name that means "the place of the olive press"). Just as a huge millstone crushes the olives in order for the olive oil to flow, so Jesus was pressed by a crisis of obedience. Would he be faithful to his heavenly Father or would he take the easy road of escape? Jesus prayed the night before his execution, seeking to be delivered from the agony that he saw coming the next day. I'm glad—aren't you?—that Jesus said yes to obedience. But see very clearly that Jesus' most difficult challenge was being obedient to his Father's plan.

And so it will be with us. The toughest bout you and I will face is not saying no to a profitable career but saying yes to a divine prompting. It is not saying no to happiness but saying yes to holiness. It is not saying no to temptation but saying yes to righteousness. Please understand that God's desire is not that we be miserable; he does want to give us the desires of our hearts. But saying yes to God's leadership can be toilsome.

Wrestling with God is the most difficult battle we will face.

We Often Try to Throw Off Our Greatest Blessings

My wife and I like to visit antique stores. Sometimes after examining the merchandise, I say to myself, *I've thrown away better stuff than this.*

My oldest brother collected baseball cards as a youngster. He had a large collection including greats Mickey Mantle, Joe DiMaggio and Ted Williams. A few years ago, when he realized that these old cards were of value beyond the bubble gum that came in the original wrapper, he searched for them in the attic of our parents' home. When he could not find them, he asked Mother if she knew what had happened to the cards. "Oh, I threw those worthless things away when you went off to college!"

The first car I ever owned was a 1968 fire-engine-red Mustang fastback. My brother and I bought it for $1,000—$500 each. We sold it for $400 a few years later. Now it is probably worth ten times that much.

The underlying truth in each of these incidents is that often one can't tell the difference between trash and treasure.

That truth also applies to our spiritual lives. All too often I can't correctly interpret what's going on in my life. It is difficult to make sense of all the pain and trials that come my way. Sometimes I can't tell if what's happening to me is a blessing or a curse, especially if I am in the midst of a crisis.

When I was playing basketball in high school, I collided with a teammate during a game. He came out of the collision barely scathed. I, on the other hand, had busted my lip, and my two front teeth were dislodged, with one hanging on by the nerve. I was rushed to a dentist, who stitched up my lip and put my teeth back where they belonged.

What appeared to be a horrible accident actually turned out to be a blessing. Before that night there was a noticeable gap between my two front teeth—a gap I did not particularly like. In fact I often hid my smile, embarrassed by the opening. When the dentist repositioned my teeth, he was able to align them so there was no gap. I walked away from his office with a bruised face, stitches in my lip and a new smile.

Jacob's story was no different. Overpowered from the rear, he couldn't tell at the moment of encounter if the struggle was to develop him or to destroy him. But in the midst of this wrestling match a pivotal point occurred. As in an athletic contest the momentum changed. "When the man saw that he could not overpower him [Jacob], he touched the socket of Jacob's hip so that his hip was wrenched as he wrestled with the man. Then the man said, 'Let me go, for it is daybreak.' But Jacob replied, 'I will not let you go unless you bless me' " (Genesis 32:25-26).

Jacob had a divine revelation. Maybe it comes to us all at some point in our lives. Jacob realized that it was in the struggle that the blessing comes. He shouldn't throw the struggle off and cast it away as trash. Treasure existed beneath the toil. Jacob realized that faith is not changing things the way we want them to be; real faith is having the courage to face the things the way they are.

Many people forgo the battle when faced with a challenge—and thereby miss the blessing. They miss God's touch because they give up too soon. I witness this struggle in my own life virtually every week.

One of the most challenging parts of my job is to prepare, write and deliver sermons. Sermon preparation is hard work. I liken it to preparing a Thanksgiving meal. The one big difference is that Thanksgiving comes around only every 365 days; Sundays come around every seven days. Some weeks I want to short-circuit the process and thereby shortchange my work. I want to skip over the hard work of diving into a subject or text to glean the truths of God's Word. It would be easier to plagiarize someone else's material by logging on to a sermon website or by pulling out a sermon journal. But I have discovered that in doing so I miss the blessings of God. My congregation may not be able to tell when I short-circuit the process, but I can tell it. Some of God's priceless treasures come at the end of the week, in the dark night of my struggle, at the conclusion of the study.

A man once found a cocoon on a tree in his back yard. He was intrigued and decided to watch it develop. One day he saw a tiny butterfly inside the delicate covering and watched it struggling, trying its best to break out of captivity. Finally the man became so frustrated that he decided to use a razorblade to make a slit in the cocoon in order to free the struggling butterfly. Soon afterward the butterfly was free, but it could not fly because the struggle to break free was the way God had designed for its beautiful wings to grow and develop. As a result it died prematurely.

It is often through our struggles that we obtain strength. It is often in our testing that we are blessed. If we short-circuit the process, we often forfeit God's greatest blessings.

When We Confess Who We Are, We Find Out Who God Wants Us to Be

The angel asked Jacob, "What is your name?" (Genesis 32:27). In the Hebrew language the questioner was not asking, "Who are you?" but "What are you?" He was not asking for information but for a confession. God wanted Jacob to admit who he was.

Jacob came out of his mother's womb holding his brother by the heel. The name Jacob means "he who catches by the heel" (or figuratively, "he deceives"). It is the same word used in Jeremiah 17:9: "The heart is deceitful above all things." The name Jacob, then, conjures up a picture of deceit, fraud and cheating. Interestingly, it pictures someone who sneaks up behind you. Jacob was a cheater, a con artist. He had cheated Esau out of his birthright and his blessing. To this point in his life, Jacob had lived up to his name.

God often asks me, "What is your name?" Or better yet, "What are you?" I don't like answering that question, because when I examine my heart, I don't see the image of myself that I try to project. I'm a sinner. I think bad thoughts. I manipulate people to get my way. I stretch the truth to make myself look good. I have perfectionist tendencies, hoping people will like me for what I do. I feel that I am not a person whom people would like for who I am. I am flawed. I don't like to admit it, but I am.

Alcoholics Anonymous and other rehabilitation programs have learned the value of confession in people's recovery. Only when people admit they are alcoholics or have an addiction can they take the steps to complete healing and lasting change.

Until we honestly face our past and admit our faults and confess our sins, God's work may be limited in our lives. God begins the change process when we first admit that we've got a problem.

We Don't Want to Be Changed As Much As God Wants to Change Us

As long as it is superficial change we're talking about, I'm okay with it. A little cosmetic surgery is fine. Any more than that and I'm uncomfortable. I'm like Wilbur Rees, who wrote, "I would like to buy $3 worth of God, please, not enough to explode my soul or disturb my sleep, but just enough to equal a cup of warm milk or a snooze in the sunshine. I don't want enough of him to make me love a black man or pick beets with a migrant. I want ecstasy, not transformation; I want the warmth of the womb, not a new birth. I want a pound of the Eternal in a paper sack. I would like to buy $3 worth of God, please."[2]

But God has different ideas. While I'm content with superficial changes, God wants to make monumental changes. While I'm satisfied with cosmetic surgery, God wants to perform radical surgery. God wants to reach down into the gut of my existence and change me into his image. He wants to reach down into the basement of my soul and perform a mira-

While I'm satisfied with cosmetic surgery, God wants to perform radical surgery.

cle. I want to work on the exterior of my charisma, while God wants to work on the interior of my character.

God wanted to change Jacob. In fact the angel said, "Your name will no longer be Jacob, but Israel, because you have struggled with God and with men and have overcome" (Genesis 32:28). As the name Jacob was significant in his past life, so the name Israel played a significant role in his new life. Israel means "he who struggles with God," or literally, "God prevails." Jacob had been changed from a deceiver into the prince of God.

After we have had a personal encounter with God, we can no longer be the same. God knew Jacob's potential; he saw beneath his exterior of trying to be a worldly wise tough guy. God saw all of Jacob's weaknesses, but he also saw beneath the surface and saw what Jacob could become. God saw the prince in Jacob, and the former cheater began to become the man for whom the entire nation of Israel was named.

In that one act of grace God set Jacob free to be Israel. That's how God works in our lives too. I am reminded of Michelangelo being asked how he could sculpt such beautiful statues. He pointed to an angel he had just completed and said, "I saw the angel in the marble and I chiseled until I set it free." God sees a person of character within you and me. He wants to set us free, like he did for Jacob. He will chisel and cut anything that's not right until he changes our cold, lifeless existence and sets us free to be the persons he desires us to be.

We Need a Constant Reminder of God's Work in Our Lives

"Then [God] blessed [Jacob] there. So Jacob called the place Peniel, saying, 'It is because I saw God face to face, and yet my life was spared.' The sun rose above him as he passed Peniel, and he was limping because of his hip" (Genesis 32:29-31). Jacob was given a new name and a new blessing, but he was also given another reminder of his encounter with God. The Lord gave Jacob a limp as well—a physical souvenir from their wrestling match. This limp would prick him every time he took a step. It would be a constant reminder of God's grace. God could have destroyed Jacob, but instead God chose to change him into a new person. He had to break his will and wrench his hip, but he got the job done.

This story is unusual even by biblical standards. God is not known for participating with men in physical contests. But the most surprising part of the episode is that God "could not overpower him" (Genesis 32:25). What does that mean? You and I both know that God could have annihilated Jacob just by speaking the word!

This scene makes sense if, besides grappling with God, Jacob was also grappling with his sinfulness that night. The Lord did not pin Jacob to the mat because he never forces anyone to surrender; he leaves our free will intact. God was dealing with a son, not a slave, and he wanted Jacob to face up to his sin by crossing the river to face his brother—not dragged there bound against his will, but walking freely.

Freely—yet with a limp. Scripture tells us that Jacob went the next day to meet Esau, and on that day he was saved from retribution.

I can picture Jacob shuffling toward Esau the morning after the wrestling match. His clothes are torn and dirty; his hair is messed up; he is walking with a limp.

"What happened to you?" Esau asks.

"I've been blessed," Jacob says. (Not the picture of a victorious believer that most often comes to our mind, but a fitting portrait of a man who has allowed God to shape and fashion his life.)

"But you are limping."

"Yes. Isn't it great?"

The limp would remind Jacob of his deceitfulness with Esau and his rebellion against God. The name Israel would be a personal reminder of the continual striving that is necessary to walk in holiness.

Jacob was a marked man. His limp was not just a sign for him; others would notice the way he walked. They probably concluded that he was a veteran of some battle. And he was.

It was not a loser's limp. It was the limp of a spiritually mature man who had come face to face with God. It proclaimed, "I lost the battle with God, but I won the war over myself." It would prick him every time he took a step. It would keep him from boasting. It would be a persistent whisper in his ear, "I saw God face to face, and yet my life was spared" (Genesis 32:30).

One sees a similar limp in those who have met God face to face. It reveals itself in various ways.

In humility. God says, "The way up is down, and the way down is up."

In service. In God's plan one does not ascend into greatness but rather one *descends* into greatness.

In pain. No pain, no gain. No guts, no glory. In fact the fullness of life does not involve the avoidance of pain but rather the courage to move through pain.

In obedience. One who is committed to Jesus does what he commands and follows where he leads.

Some people would have walked away from that experience with only a limp and never have changed. They would have named the place "This is where I got hurt" or "Place of misfortune." Jacob, instead, named this piece of real estate "The place where I met God face to face."

What do we call the places where we have wrestled with God? God wants us to see those places in a new light and put a marker at that point as the place where we met God and were forever changed.

The greatest change does not occur in a single event but over a lifetime. Change is a process. Change can be our friend. Change in God's plan is always a struggle to the breaking of the day. The change we desire may seem to take too long for us or seem too hard to accomplish. But no person is too far gone for God. Change is no easy task, but for God it is all in a night's work.

When our sins catch up with us, we can do one of two things: run or wrestle. Many choose to run. But the best way to deal with our past is to face it head-on. No more denial. No more pretending. No more repression. We need to battle God face to face and hope that we lose.

A friend was teasing his buddy, who had misspent most of his life. He asked mischievously, "Say, John, you still spending a lot of time wrestling with the old devil?"

The fellow answered good-naturedly, "Nowadays I spend most of my time wrestling with God."

His friend asked incredulously, "Wrestling with God? How do you hope to win a wrestling match with God?"

John smiled and answered, "Oh, you misunderstand. In this wrestling match I'm hoping to lose."

Me too.

Study Questions

1. How does the world's definition of success differ from the Bible's definition of success?

2. What goes through your mind when you are about to meet someone you have not seen in many years?

3. Respond to the statement "God comes into our lives not only to comfort our affliction but also to arouse us from a state of complacency."

4. Why is it often harder to say yes to God than to say no to the devil?

5. Describe a time when a struggle in your life produced blessing.

6. If God asked you, as he did Jacob, "What is your name?" (meaning "What are you?" not "Who are you?"), what would you say?

7. "While I'm satisfied with cosmetic surgery, God wants to perform radical surgery." In what ways does God need to radically change your life?

8. God gave Jacob a limp, reminding him of his encounter. What physical souvenirs do you have of wrestling with the divine?

9. Are you in a period of radical change? How could this change be one of your defining moments?

Three

When You Can't See God

I n the film *Jerry Maguire* Cuba Gooding Jr. plays an exuberant pro football receiver who stays loyal to newly independent agent Jerry Maguire, played by Tom Cruise. In the show-stopping scene in which Jerry is trying to convince the receiver that he can represent him well, Gooding's character wants to make sure it is not all talk, so he says to Jerry, "Show me the money." Over and over again he repeats, "Show me the money." He has Jerry repeat the phrase: "Show me the money. Show me the money."

Not unlike Gooding's character, I want to be shown. Like my friends from Missouri, the "Show Me State," just show me. I bought a garage door opener this past summer. The salesperson was telling me how to install it. In the middle of the explanation I wanted to scream, "Don't tell me; show me!" A few months ago, when trying to find a hospital in Chicago, I asked for directions. As the cabby was telling me the different streets I had to travel, my heart was saying, "Don't tell me; show me!" At the pool a few summers ago my daughter wanted to learn how to dive into the water. "How do I do it, Daddy?" Reclining in my chaise longue with a thermos of ice water and a book on my lap, I explained to her, "Honey, you put your arms over your head, bend your knees and thrust your body into the water headfirst." Exasperated and confused, she cried, "Daddy, don't tell me. Get up. Show me."

Blurred Vision

On the first Easter morning Mary of Magdala was just as exasperated and confused. She had walked to the tomb where Jesus had been buried. Upon arriving at the grave, she discovered that the stone had been rolled away and the body of Jesus was gone. Hear her exasperation. To Simon Peter and John, she lamented, "They have taken the Lord out of the tomb, and *we don't know where they have put him!*" (John 20:2, emphasis added). To the two angels outside the tomb, she said, "They have taken my Lord away, and *I don't know where they have put him*" (verse 13, emphasis added). In her own way she was screaming, "Show me! Please, show me where they have put him."

Who were "they"?

She was confused: Did grave robbers steal the body? Did the soldiers dispose of the body? Did some disciples move the body? For Mary there were more questions than answers, more tears than laughter.

I can hear her cry: "Where's Jesus? Show me Jesus. Who has taken him? Why? When can I see him? Is this it? Are there no last respects I can pay? Show me Jesus. Can't I see him one more time? Can't I caress his face again? Can't I kiss his cheek? Show me Jesus."

It had been an emotional weekend. Mary's dreams were shattered when Jesus was crucified. No wonder "Mary stood outside the tomb crying" (John 20:11).

I would have cried too. I know what it is like to have dreams shattered, hope destroyed and joy crushed. I know what it is like to be up for an award and not receive it. I know what it is like to throw one's entire self into a project, just to see it end in failure. I know what it is like to come close to fulfilling a dream, only to miss it. I know what it is like to have friends and parents die.

On a cold December night in 1983 I received a phone call that woke me from my sleep. As a pastor, I hate receiving calls in the middle of the night—it's never good news. Good news can wait, but not bad news. I did not have time to contemplate what it might be—a church member in jail, a teenager run away, an emergency at the hospital. When I answered the phone, it was not what I expected. It had nothing to do with my church family; it had to do with my family and me.

The voice on the other end of the phone belonged to the pastor of my parents' church. "Rick, your father has had a heart attack."

"Well, is he okay?" I questioned.

"Rick, (pause) he has passed away."

The phone slipped from my hand and tears came to my eyes. My daddy died when I was twenty-seven. True, he had lived a long and healthy life, but he would not hold my daughter in his arms. He would not attend my doctoral graduation. He would not observe me as pastor of a church. He would not hold in his hands the books I had written. My tears blurred my vision.

I relived those emotions fourteen years later. I found myself in the waiting room of a hospital in Huntsville, Alabama. I was not there because I was a pastor. Granted, I have spent my fair share of time at hospitals doing my duty. This time, though, I was there because I was a son, and my mother, at eighty-three years of age, was lying in the bed of room six of the Cardiac Care Unit on the sixth floor with tubes running in and out of her body. She was dying.

For the three years prior, she had been in and out of the hospital every other month due to congestive heart failure. My two brothers and two sisters and I knew that this time was the most frightening. The night before I had left my home in Chicago to fly to Alabama, her heart had stopped. Through the valiant efforts of the nursing staff, it was restarted.

On Sunday morning, September 21, 1997, ten days after I had arrived in Alabama, my mother's heart stopped beating. The nurses, per their instructions, did not resuscitate her. She slipped through the chains of death and entered a new life in heaven.

When I received the news, I walked away from my family to look out a window. My daughter jumped in my arms. I held her tightly and cried. The tears flowed easily. Someone I cared for deeply was gone. I had lost my confidante, my encourager, my friend. But most of all I had lost my mother.

I was sad. I was hurt. I wanted to shout and scream, but all I could do was cry. And as I cried, my vision was blurred. Tears have a way of distorting things, like a glass of water into which a straw has been inserted. You can see the straw, but it appears bent. In relation to my mother's death, there were some things I couldn't make sense of. I was confused.

That's what happened to Mary. She, too, had come face to face with death, and her tears blurred her vision. Outside the tomb in the garden she encountered Jesus, but she didn't recognize him. She looked in the wrong direction. " 'Woman,' he said, 'why are you crying? Who is it you are looking for?' Thinking he was the gardener, she said, 'Sir, if you have carried him away, tell me *where you have put him,* and I will get him.' Jesus said to her, 'Mary' " (John 20:15-16, emphasis added). The voice. It was the voice of Jesus. It jolted her out of despair. Dreams began to take shape. Hope rang out. Joy filled her soul. Her tears were transformed into rivers of laughter. Her confusion was reborn into fountains of understanding. And her exasperation flowed away into pools of living water. She had wanted to see Jesus, and she did. Her prayer of "Show me Jesus" had been answered. He was standing in front of her breathing and talking. He was alive.

In her crisis of confusion Jesus brought understanding. It was her defining moment. Jesus erased the tears with comfort. He removed her confusion and replaced it with clarity. He dispelled her fear with faith. He renewed her despondency with hope. In one climactic moment she saw her Savior and he was alive.

Seeing Jesus has that effect on me too. That day my mother died on the sixth floor of Huntsville Hospital, I saw Jesus in the face of my wife, my daughter and my family. He brought joy and peace to a life that had known death and despair. He healed my broken heart. He transformed my wayward soul, bent on confusion and exasperation, into one full of purpose and hope. Seeing Jesus enabled me to sing, in the words of the great old gospel song,

> And he walks with me, and he talks with me, and he tells me I am his own;
> and the joy we share as we tarry there, none other has ever known.[1]

I can't explain it, but I know he was there. The thought of Jesus alive brought wonder to my soul and calmness to my mind.

That joy can't be boxed up and tucked away in the recesses of our hearts. That joy has to get out. Like exploding fireworks on the Fourth of July, it lights up the sky for all to see and hear. It's like winning an Oscar at the Academy Awards and calling everybody to tell them about it. Or having the Publisher's Clearing House prize patrol come to our house to announce that we are the grand prize winner and then throwing a party for all our family and friends. Or giving birth to a child and calling everybody we know to share the wonderful news. Good news is for sharing.

And that's just what Mary did. "Mary Magdalene went to the disciples with the news: 'I have seen the Lord!' " (John 20:18). Mary had made more than a visual identification. Something had clicked within her, as it did with all the other disciples. A light had come on. Jesus' words of death and resurrection now made sense. He had told them; now he showed them. He was alive just as he had said.

An old story tells of a company attempting to start a new pension plan, which required 100-percent participation. Every employee signed up except one. No amount of argument or persuasion could get this person to change his mind. Finally the president of the company called the unwilling man into his office. "Here is a copy of the proposed pension plan and here is a pen," he said. "Sign up or you're fired." Whereupon the employee immediately picked up the pen and signed his name. The president of the company then said, "I don't understand why you refused to sign until now. What was your problem?" The man replied, "You're the first person who showed it to me so clearly."

That's what Jesus did for Mary. He showed her clearly what he had come to do. Her confusion was made clear.

Christ Went to a Tomb

The location of Jesus' tomb is no longer known with certainty. But one spot in Jerusalem that some have identified as the place is called the Garden Tomb. From this site you can see what many believe to be Golgotha—the Place of the Skull, located just outside the Jerusalem wall. Close by is a bus depot. Hundreds of thousands of tourists walk about as though nothing of importance may have occurred on that spot. Just outside the grounds you can see mobile telephone towers, smell diesel fumes and witness tourists scurrying from one place to another. The garden area itself is quiet and peaceful—at least when throngs of tourists are not crowding around to take photos.

The garden is beautiful. The tomb has had some concrete blocks inserted in its outer wall due to earthquake damage years ago. A small opening to the tomb has a trough for a stone to cover the opening. It is a rock-hewn tomb four feet high and four feet wide, with three steps across the rock floor to the other side. The rock bed would have been cold and rough. A place of death, not a place for tourists, housed the body of Christ.

God entered into a dark, claustrophobic room. He allowed soldiers to seal it shut. The light of the world was shut away in darkness. The hope of humanity was shut up in helplessness.

Jesus died for us. Yes, he died for us. Allow those words to sink in for a moment.

The Tomb Was a Prison

This tomb was more than a place of burial; it was a place of punishment. Maybe we can't visualize the tomb where Jesus was buried. But we can picture in our mind's eye another place—a prison cell. The tomb where Jesus was buried was like a cold, dark and lonely prison cell.

Your sin and mine put Jesus in prison. In heaven's plan someone had to die. Either it would be God's only Son or it would be us. Jesus took our spot in that place of punishment. He paid the price for our sin.

Near the city of São José dos Campos, Brazil, is a remarkable facility. Twenty years ago the Brazilian government turned a prison over to two Christians. The institution was renamed Humaita, and the plan was to run it on Christian principles. With the exception of two full-time staff, inmates do all the work. Families outside the prison adopt an inmate to work with during and after his term. Chuck Colson visited the prison and made this report:

> When I visited Humaita I found the inmates smiling—particularly the murderer who held the keys, opened the gates, and let me in. Wherever I walked I saw men at peace. I saw clean living areas, people working industriously. The walls were decorated with biblical sayings from Psalms and Proverbs. . . .

My guide escorted me to the notorious punishment cell once used for torture. Today, he told me, that block houses only a single inmate. As we reached the end of a long concrete corridor and he put the key into the lock, he paused and asked, "Are you sure you want to go in?"

"Of course," I replied impatiently. "I've been in isolation cells all over the world." Slowly he swung open the massive door, and I saw the prisoner in that punishment cell: a crucifix, beautifully carved by the Humaita inmates—the prisoner Jesus, hanging on the cross.

"He's doing time for all the rest of us," my guide said softly.[2]

Christ has taken our place. He's doing the time we deserve. We are discharged from the penitentiary of sin.

Why would we live as a prisoner when we have the possibility of freedom? Why would we prefer death to life? Why would we live under bondage when the penalty has been paid?

> Why would we live as a prisoner when we have the possibility of freedom?

The Prison Is Empty

Whether the tomb of Christ is found in the Garden Tomb or in Jerusalem's Church of the Holy Sepulchre or a long-forgotten hole in the ground, it is empty. Mary found an empty tomb on that first Easter morning. The empty tomb signifies that Jesus is alive. Then. Now. Forever.

I suppose what follows is a true story. Regardless, its truth pierces my heart and causes me to cry happy tears.

Jeremy was born with a twisted body and a slow mind. At the age of twelve he was still in second grade, seemingly unable to learn. His teacher, Doris Miller, often became exasperated with him. He would squirm in his seat, drool and make grunting noises.

At other times he spoke clearly and distinctly, as if a ray of light had penetrated the darkness of his brain. Most of the time, however, Jeremy irritated his teacher. She had eighteen other youngsters to teach, and Jeremy was a distraction. Furthermore, he would never learn to read and write. Why waste any more time trying?

She prayed for more patience with Jeremy.

Spring came and the children talked excitedly about the coming of Easter. Doris told them the story of Jesus, and then, to emphasize the idea of new life springing forth, she gave each of the children a large plastic egg. "Now," she said to them, "I want you to take this home and bring it back tomorrow with something inside that shows new life. Do you understand?"

"Yes, Miss Miller!" the children responded enthusiastically—all except Jeremy. He just listened intently; his eyes never leaving her face. He did not even make his usual noises.

The next morning, nineteen children came to school, laughing and talking as they placed their eggs in the large wicker basket on Miss Miller's desk. After they completed their math lesson, it was time to open the eggs.

In the first egg Doris found a flower. "Oh yes, a flower is certainly a sign of new life," she said. A small girl in the first row waved her arm. "That's my egg, Miss Miller," she called out.

The next egg contained a plastic butterfly, which looked very real. Doris held it up. "We all know that a caterpillar changes and grows into a beautiful butterfly. Yes, that is new life too." Little Judy smiled proudly and said, "Miss Miller, that one is mine!"

Next, Doris found a rock with moss on it. She explained that moss, too, showed life. Billy spoke up from the back of the classroom: "My Daddy helped me!"

Then Doris opened the fourth egg. She gasped. The egg was empty! Surely it must be Jeremy's, she thought, for of course he had not understood her instructions. If only she had not forgotten to phone his parents! Because she did not want to embarrass him, she quietly set the egg aside and reached for another.

Suddenly Jeremy spoke up. "Miss Miller, aren't you going to talk about my egg?"

Flustered, Doris replied, "But Jeremy, your egg is empty!"

He looked into her eyes and said softly, "Yes, but Jesus' tomb was empty too!"

Time stopped. When she could speak again, Doris asked him, "Do you know why the tomb was empty?"

"Oh yes!" Jeremy said. "Jesus was killed and put in there. Then his Father raised him up!"

The recess bell rang. While the children excitedly ran out to the school yard, Doris cried. The ice inside her melted completely away.

Three months later Jeremy died. Those who paid their respects at the mortuary were surprised to see nineteen eggs on top of the casket, all of them empty.[3]

And the power that emptied that tomb, raising Jesus to life, is the same power that propels us beyond the grip of earth's atmosphere to an eternal home with the Father.

Jeremy knew it. Mary saw it. And we can experience it.

When we are shown the love that enabled Jesus to go to a tomb, when we are shown the logic that enabled Jesus to pay the price for our sin, and when we are shown the power that enabled Jesus to rise from the dead, then we can have only one response—thankfulness. That's what Easter is all about. It is about a tomb that is empty, a price that was paid for our sin. It is about a thankful heart.

When I was nine years old, the love and logic and power of Easter made sense. I was reared in a devout Christian home. In our family, church attendance was not optional. I heard all the Bible stories. I knew all the right answers. But the recesses of my soul were dark. I saw, but I did not see. My mother showed Jesus to me; she explained the story of Jesus in a way that made sense. The light went on. I saw Jesus. It was a defining moment in my life. I am forever thankful. And like Mary, one day I will fall at the feet of Jesus to say thanks for helping me to see and to understand him.

Study Questions

1. In what areas of life do you prefer to be shown—not told—how to do something?

2. If you were with Mary, expecting to see the body of Jesus and finding the tomb empty, how would you have responded?

3. If you have had someone close to you die, how did you feel?

4. Visualize a prison cell and put yourself behind bars. How do you feel about being locked up, serving a sentence for a crime that you did not commit?

5. Describe the first time you comprehended what Jesus did for you on the cross.

6. Describe the emotions associated with understanding that Jesus' tomb is empty.

7. In what ways do you express your thankfulness for the empty tomb?

Four

When You Are
Visited by God

I grew up in a small town in northern Alabama. Our home was located just off Main Street with the bank on one side and the Baptist church on the other. Behind our house was an acre of trees my twin brother, Micky, and I simply called "the woods." In those woods we played cowboys and Indians, camped out, went exploring and built forts. When we found road kill—opossums, squirrels, raccoons and the like—we would string them up on a tree. I don't know why; we just did. Between our back yard and the woods, Daddy had a small garden.

One fall afternoon when I was eight or nine, Micky and I began piling up the dried cornstalks from the garden. We had a pretty tall stack when Micky said, "Wouldn't it be fun to see those things burn?" I had found a box of matches earlier in the day, so Micky said, "Why don't you light the pile? Nothing will happen. Mother will never find out." I was old enough to doubt his assurances, but my curiosity got the better of me. So I lighted those dried leaves and in just a few minutes the pile was consumed by an inferno. Before we could think to douse the fire with water, it had spread. Now the entire garden was in flames. And the woods stood in the path of the ever-growing fire.

"Go get the water hose!" I yelled to Micky.

"You started it; you go get the hose!" he shouted back.

We stood wide-eyed in wonder just yards away, mesmerized by the dancing flames that crackled and popped as they were now spreading into the woods. We stood transfixed, nearly oblivious to the searing heat, until Mother came rushing from the house, screaming for us to move back to safety.

Soon people from town were coming to watch. Others pulled up in their cars to the bank and church parking lots to see the blaze. I wanted to get lost for a week. Fortunately someone had the good sense to call the volunteer fire department and they put out the fire before all of the woods was destroyed.

After the fire was extinguished and the crowd had disbanded, my mother asked who had started the fire. I did the brave and noble thing. I said, "Micky did."

Eventually I confessed. Later that year Daddy had a man come with his bulldozer and remove the small trees and underbrush from our woods. Daddy said it was because he wanted a bigger garden. Micky said it was because he got tired of smelling dead opossums hanging from the trees. I think it was because I almost burned the entire town to the ground.

I learned some important lessons from this experience. One, don't play with matches. Two, don't do everything your brother tells you to do. Three, mothers always find out. And four, fire consumes, spreads and attracts a whole lot of people.

The Consuming Fire of God

I imagine that it was on a beautiful fall day that Solomon and the people of Israel came together to dedicate the temple. They had worked long and hard to build a permanent and magnificent structure to house the Ark of the Covenant. Finally the day had arrived for the temple dedication. The people gathered and Solomon prayed. "When Solomon finished praying, fire came down from heaven and consumed the burnt offering and the sacrifices, and the glory of the LORD filled the temple" (2 Chronicles 7:1). I don't know about Solomon, but if I were in his shoes, this would have been an unforgettable experience—a defining moment.

The thought of fire falling from the sky boggles my mind. I know what fire can do to some cornstalks. In my wildest dreams I cannot imagine what it would be like witnessing God's igniting the sacrifices on an altar.

God has always used fire as a way of identifying his presence. To Moses, God spoke through a burning bush. To Elijah, God consumed an altar with fire from heaven. To the first few believers in Jerusalem, God visited them in the form of a violent blowing wind and tongues of fire. To Solomon and the worshipers at the temple, God came as a fire from heaven consuming the sacrifices.

When God spoke to Moses through the burning bush, he was saying that the place where Moses was standing was holy ground. When the fire fell on the altar that Elijah had built, God was proclaiming, among other things, that this was a holy man. When God visited the early followers of Christ with tongues of fire, he was announcing that these were a holy people. And when the fire fell in the temple Solomon had built, God was stating that this was a holy place. The consuming fire was God's presence making something holy. Only God can do that.

Cliff Barrows, a long-time associate of Billy Graham, tells of going with his dad to Yosemite National Park years ago. They toured the park all day, in awe of the majestic valley and its surroundings. At the end of the day the forest ranger who was leading their group took them to the ridge called Glacier Point. Darkness was falling. Across from them stood a sheer face of rock over a thousand feet high. The ranger said that since early morning men had been burning timber above the cliff, and they could see huge piles of white-hot coals all along the rim.

As the last rays of light receded from the horizon, a ranger at the top of the cliff called to the small group down on Glacier Point, "Are you ready?" Cliff said the ranger's voice echoed through the valley in a way that sent chills down his spine. The guide near him looked up and answered, "We are ready! Let the fire fall!"

At that moment the men high on the cliff began to shovel the hot coals over the side, the coals bursting into flame as they hit the cool night air. For several minutes this continued, and the group watched in wonder as a fiery wall over a thousand feet high and a hundred yards wide lit the night sky. No one moved. No one spoke. Mesmerized, they watched the fire fall.

When the fire falls on our lives, be it personally or corporately, all we can do is fall to the ground and worship a holy and living God. Worshiping in awe, we are mesmerized by the sight of his consuming glory and grace. That's what the people of Israel did. "When all the Israelites saw the fire coming down and the glory of the LORD above the temple, they knelt on the pavement with their faces to the ground, and they worshiped and gave thanks to the LORD" (2 Chronicles 7:3). Worship is expressing our love to God for who he is, what he's said and what he's doing. In genuine worship the warmth of God's presence is felt, the cleansing of God's pardon is offered, the burning of God's purposes is seen, and the flame of God's power is displayed.

> Worship does not *lead* to an encounter with God; it *is* an encounter with God.

Worship is not a weekly pep talk to rally the troops in order to win the contest. Worship is not the Christian's alternative to a Saturday night rock concert. Worship occurs when people who have fallen in love with the God of the universe meet him in his consuming glory. Worship does not *lead* to an encounter with God; it *is* an encounter with God.

The Spreading Fire of God

The nature of fire is to consume. Its nature is also to spread. God not only wants his presence to consume us, resulting in our worship; he also wants his fire to spread into the hearts of others. Worship without witness is spiritual abortion. Witness without worship is religious suicide. There is an intimate connection between worship and witnessing. It is the goal of our witnessing to produce worshipers of God. And at the same time, it is worship that provides the motivation for witnessing. Worship produces a desire in us to tell others about Christ.

God said to Solomon, "If my people, who are called by my name, will humble themselves and pray and seek my face and turn from their wicked ways, then I will hear from heaven and will forgive their sin and will heal their land" (2 Chronicles 7:14). *If* is the biggest two-letter word in the

English language. The destiny of persons, families and nations hinges on that one little word. This statement was a word from God to Solomon following the temple dedication ceremony. The temple symbolized commitment to worship and partnership with God. *If* suggests responsibility on the hearer's part. God was saying to Solomon, "You are the man to carry my flame into the world." And to the nation of Israel he was saying, "You are the people. The responsibility of proclaiming my forgiveness and healing is yours."

The responsibility for spreading the flame of God's forgiveness and healing rests squarely on the hearer's shoulders. Just as God was saying to Solomon, "You are the man," so he is saying to you and me, "You are the man! You are the woman!" Just as God was saying to the people of Israel, "You are the people," so he is saying to every Christian church, "You are the people!" When the fire falls on us, we are compelled to burn for others. If the fire would fall on others, our hearts have to burn.

In 1949 Dr. Henrietta Mears of Hollywood Presbyterian Church had been conducting a collegiate conference. Several committed men joined her one night for prayer. In the midst of that prayer meeting God touched all of them in a unique way. Their hearts began to glow with the flame of God. During that prayer meeting, one discouraged pastor entered late, intending to tell Dr. Mears that he was leaving the ministry. Upon joining the group, he too was touched by the fire of God and found fresh meaning, purpose and power in life. Because God had touched them, they wanted to call others to join them in prayer. They formed what they called the "Fellowship of the Burning Heart," which was committed to calling others to join them in prayer and work for spreading the fire of God in the world. The results were amazing.

After that meeting, Dr. Bill Bright founded Campus Crusade for Christ. Today its full-time staff numbers more than 21,900 in 186 countries around the world, spreading the flame of God's message. Millions have found Christ through this movement.

Dr. Louis Evans Jr. later became pastor of the National Presbyterian Church in Washington, D.C., where he ministered to thousands.

The discouraged pastor, Richard Halverson, stayed in the ministry and pastored the Fourth Presbyterian Church in Washington. He also was chaplain of the U.S. Senate, providing spiritual counsel to many who held high office in our land.

When their hearts burned with the fire of God's presence, they could not contain the spreading fire of God's forgiveness and healing.

We used to speak of those Christ followers passionate about sharing their faith as being "on fire." Could it be that we don't say that phrase today because so few are on fire?

What will it take for us to be set on fire? Fire cannot be ignited when it is in an environment that is hostile to combustion. To be on fire, we must be composed of combustible material. We must find a way to create a kind of spiritual reaction that creates both heat and light. And that way is no secret. God gives us the formula for starting a fire in our hearts. Actually it is as simple as striking a match and lighting a pile of dried cornhusks. The way is found in 2 Chronicles 7:14. "If" shows our responsibility. "Humble themselves" shows the direction of our heart—toward God. "Pray" shows the direction of our words—toward God. "Seek my face" shows the direction of our ambition—toward God. "Turn from their wicked ways" shows the direction of our walk—toward God.

When we start living with our hearts, words, ambition and walk directed toward God, we will be changed. The spark of God's passion will ignite within us. A spontaneous combustion of a higher kind will result. The flames of our witness will become like an uncontrollable grass fire spreading into the hearts and lives of people around us.

Are we combustible people? Are we allowing God to strike the match to set our dry hearts ablaze with his energy, power and love? Would that each of us would be as Jim Elliot when he prayed:

> God deliver me from the dread asbestos of other things. Saturate me with the oil of the Spirit that I may be aflame. . . . Father, take my life, yea, my blood if Thou wilt, and consume it with Thine enveloping fire. I would not save it for it is not mine to save. Have it, Lord, have it all. Pour out my life as an oblation for the world. . . . Make me Thy fuel, Flame of God.[1]

When we see the fire fall on our hearts, all we can do is witness to its source and power.

The Cleansing Fire of God

The consuming fire of God compels us to worship. The spreading fire of God leads us to witness. But it is the cleansing fire of God that washes us pure. When we are responsive to God's directive, then we can claim God's promise: "Then will I hear from heaven and will forgive their sin and will heal their land" (2 Chronicles 7:14). God's hearing and forgiveness and healing result in our cleansing.

Standing beneath the giant sequoias in King's Canyon National Park, the forest ranger told the tour group that fire is necessary for the growth and reproduction of those magnificent trees, the largest and oldest living things on planet earth. It seems that at one time the U.S. Forest Service had carefully guarded them from naturally occurring, lightning-caused forest fires, only to discover that the trees were not thriving and that no new trees were developing. They came to the conclusion that without periodic fires to burn away the underbrush the trees would fail to reproduce. It takes the intense heat of a roaring fire to open the seed cones, and the ashes contain just the right mineral mixture on which the trees thrive.

So it is with Christ's followers. Without the intense heat of God's fire, we will not thrive and grow and reproduce. Yet we think the fire will hurt (and at times it just might), so we attempt to avoid the crisis of God's cleansing fire. But as with the forest of sequoias, the fire is needed. It is through this cleansing that we feel God's love, experience God's grace and know God's comfort. To live without these manifold provisions is to limp through life with a deformed character unable to reach the heights for which we were designed.

Like the forest rangers, we need to allow God's cleansing fire to periodically occur. For it is through that fire of forgiveness that our sin debt is canceled. It is through the fiery touch of God, much like a physician cauterizing a wound, that spiritual healing occurs.

A young man, Evan Roberts, was God's instrument to ignite the great Welsh revival of 1904. Roberts prayed thirteen years for a spiritual awakening. One Monday night he spoke in a prayer meeting and seventeen young people responded. In two months seventy thousand were saved, eighty-five thousand in five months and one hundred thousand in six months. The fire of God fell. And as miraculous as these statistics are, the most compelling were the cleansing effects on society at large. Taverns closed for lack of business. The crime rate dropped radically, leaving police little to do. People paid old debts and made restitution for thefts. Work slowed down in the coal mines as the mules, accustomed to profuse profanity, had to learn the new language of the converted miners.

The cleansing fire of God fell on a people and the land experienced forgiveness and healing. May it happen again.

The Contagious Fire of God

In recent years we have seen headlines about church buildings being set on fire by arsonists. What if we saw similar headlines—"Church on fire"— because of the intensity of its worship and the passion of its witness? Wouldn't it be awe-inspiring if the fire of God's presence fell on our congregations in extraordinary measure? Wouldn't it be attractive if our churches caught fire, spreading God's message to their communities and beyond?

You know what would happen, don't you? People would come and watch us burn.

As a young boy in that small Alabama town, I would occasionally hear the fire siren atop the water tower. First, I would look around me, making sure I had not set anything else on fire. Then I would wait for the sound of the fire truck, seeing in which direction it would speed off toward a blaze. Next, something interesting would happen. A parade of cars would follow in hot pursuit of the fire truck—some to help the volunteers, but most to watch the fire.

> Christians who carry large Bibles will not attract many people, but the fire of its words that has transformed their lives will.

Like my little fire experiment revealed, fire attracts a lot of people.

Church buildings will not attract many people, but fire in the hearts of the people who worship and witness in them will. Christians who carry large Bibles will not attract many people, but the fire of its words that has transformed their lives will. Ministries that are high-tech will not attract many people, but the fire that has scorched its leaders and members, compelling them to reach out in significant ways to others, will.

Is your heart aglow? Are you on fire? Or does God need to light a match to your dried heart, rekindling a passion for him and a compassion for lost souls?

The Punishing Fire of God

The image of fire that I have portrayed to this point is a positive one. But in reality fire most often has a destructive character, if not a deadly one. I lit a match to some dried cornhusks and my childhood woods were nearly destroyed. Others, less naively, light gasoline cans in houses or light fuses to bombs or light torches to buildings, and the result is highly destructive.

God's fire is also a punishing fire. To Solomon, God issued a warning: "If you turn away and forsake the decrees and commands I have given you and go off to serve other gods and worship them, then I will uproot Israel from my land, which I have given them, and will reject this temple I have consecrated for my Name. I will make it a byword and an object of ridicule among all peoples" (2 Chronicles 7:19-20). I can imagine the voice of God reverberating through the temple as these words are being spoken. The place would be trembling like an earthquake had hit. And if Solomon was not shaking in his royal boots, he surely should have been. God wanted Solomon to know that he meant business. This was not a fluffy pat-everyone-on-the-back-for-the-good-job-they-did temple dedication service. This was serious stuff.

Somehow in our comfortable culture we long for the compassion of God but forget the judgment of God. We come to our churches, which look more like carpeted living rooms than places of worship, and expect our preachers to move around in bathrobes and slippers and speak in soft tones so as not to awaken us out of our slumber. We want our religion to make us feel good. We devise gods to make us more comfortable in our affluence and to reassure us of our status quo. We want Jesus to be a cheap therapist. We want God to love us and the Holy Spirit to be our friend.

But God wants to shake our places of worship and the people who worship him.

God is a real God, not some pale, idolatrous projection of our own ego. I've seen God allow successful businesspeople to become sick and rational corporate managers to lose control. I've seen people made to feel guilty about their behavior last weekend even in a world that lives by the philosophy "If it seems right, it is." I've seen God drive people off of ladders that ascended to the top of their professions and lead them to the mission fields of Indonesia.

William Willimon tells that at the base of the pulpit of the Duke University Chapel is a Christian symbol consisting of three triangles. It's a symbol for the triune God—Father, Son and Holy Spirit. A student on Parents' Weekend was heard to ask his dad, "Why have they got the warning symbol for nuclear radiation on the pulpit?" Sure enough, Willimon says, it *does* look like the international warning symbol for radiation. But it's not a symbol for radiation. It's a symbol for the living God.

All of our pulpits and houses of worship need a warning symbol. God is God. He is to be treated, respected and honored as God. His words are true and are to be obeyed. We are to approach him protected with spiritual lead garments because we are about to be exposed to the radiating fire of God. Left unheeded, his fire will bring about damage and destruction, if not death.

As a young boy, I learned that a fire consumes, spreads and attracts a lot of people.

May we all learn, as Solomon did in the moment that defined his life, that God's consuming fire compels us to worship. His spreading fire leads us to witness. His cleansing fire washes us pure. His contagious fire attracts a lot of people. His punishing fire issues us a warning.

May the fire of God fall on our lives once again so that we will burn for Jesus. May God's grace intervene if we don't.

Study Questions

1. Describe an event in which you witnessed a fire burning out of control.

2. Identify instances in the Bible where fire is mentioned.

3. What does it mean to be holy in the twenty-first century?

4. What do the following statements mean to you: "Worship without witness is spiritual abortion. Witness without worship is religious suicide"?

5. Describe someone you have known who was truly on fire for God. How did he or she differ from other Christians?

6. How has God's cleansing fire touched your life?

7. What do you need to do to ignite your dried heart, rekindling passion for God and compassion for lost souls?

8. In what ways have you witnessed the judgment of God in this society?

Five

When You Have to
Take a Stand

On location in Hawaii, Michael Benson, Chris Duddy and Craig Hosking—a Hollywood film crew—were filming for the thriller *Sliver*. They found themselves flying in a helicopter inside the Pu'u 'O'o crater of Kilauea, filming the world's most active volcano, erupting for the past ten years.

As the helicopter descended into the bowl of fire, hovering just ten feet above the floor of the inferno, steam and foul-smelling gases rose upward from bubbling pools of red-hot lava, obscuring vision. Suddenly the pilot shouted, "We've got a problem!" The passengers looked up just in time to see the wall of the volcano directly in front of them.

"We're dead!" yelled Duddy.

The two rotor blades hit the volcano's wall and were instantly sheared off, plunging the chopper down into the fiery pit. The helicopter landed on solid ground and the inhabitants scrambled out onto the rock. Unexpectedly they were living a thriller far more real than the one they had been filming.

Baptized into harsh fumes, Duddy and Benson tried climbing straight up the nearest wall, only to keep slipping back in the loose cinders. Eventually Benson managed to climb to a narrow ledge about seventy-five feet below the outer rim, while Duddy climbed thirty feet higher.

In the meantime Hosking got the chopper's radio working and frantically called for help. But with fog and clouds closing in, their hopes of escaping shrank. When Benson and Duddy heard the sound of a helicopter hovering overhead, they shouted to Hosking, who was not in sight. When he didn't reply, they assumed he had fallen or been overcome by the fumes. In fact, Hosking had been spotted by the helicopter and been lifted to safety. The problem for Benson and Duddy was that they were in an inaccessible spot in the volcano.

With darkness falling, Duddy and Benson realized they were going to have to spend the night clinging to ledges inside the seething volcano.

Throughout the night a ranger up on the rim blew a whistle to keep the men's spirits up. Below them, the lava lake glowed fiery red, lighting up the canyon walls. It looked like hell itself. Duddy started losing hope. He looked up at the cliff walls and concluded, "I can die trying to get out of here, or I can die waiting, curled up in a fetal position." So he said a prayer, took a deep breath and started climbing up. Against all odds, he made it to the top of the cinder wall and propelled himself over the top to safety.

Now Benson alone remained inside the volcanic crater. The whole ordeal seemed as incredible as any action movie he had filmed, only much more frightening. "I was waiting for the director to say, 'Cut,' " he said later. "But reality set in. This is not a movie. This is real, and I'm actually sitting here, dying."

That night, sleep eluded him. He lay awake with terrifying hallucinations. At one point he saw Madam Pele, the supposed fire goddess of this volcano. "All these faces of everyone I had known came by me," he said. "I heard maybe two thousand voices and every one of them said, 'You have everything to live for. You're a fighter. You're too young to die.' "

Salvation came the next morning.

Risking his own life, Maui pilot Tom Hauptman lowered his chopper into the smoldering crater and held it rock-steady. He dangled a seventy-foot cable with a chair-sized basket in Benson's vicinity. On the fourth cast

Benson grabbed hold and climbed aboard. "They lifted me out of there and gave me the ride of my life."[1]

Yes, sometimes life gets hotter than hell. Sometimes we find ourselves in a fiery furnace. Sometimes we are at a point where one more breath may be our last. Sometimes we feel like we are going to be swallowed alive. Just ask Benson, Duddy and Hosking.

Just ask Shadrach, Meshach and Abednego. These three Hebrews found themselves in a living hell. Literally. They were in the pit of an incinerator with no relief in sight. Their trial seemed to be one without any means of escape.

It is the same with you and me. Sometimes we find ourselves in a living hell. When it seems like life can't get any hotter, it does.

Maybe you've had one of those experiences. Maybe you've had a month or a year like that. A living hell. Even when you are doing the right things, you find yourself in the fire. It may be a blister on your finger or an aneurysm in your artery. It may be that you've lost your wallet or your business. It may be that you have your plans for a day ruined or your hopes for a lifetime crushed. The only guarantee in life is that from time to time life gets hotter than we like.

I recently had a bad week. Monday night my car wouldn't start. I got a ride home from work. Tuesday I thought I could get the car started myself. I couldn't. Wednesday I had the car towed to a garage. They got it started. Thursday I went to pick up the car, running late because I attended a parents' day at my daughter's school. When I got to my car, the wind chill was 35°F below zero. The snow drifts from the night before left knee-deep snow barricading my car. It took several minutes to shovel out the car. Traveling to work, I turned into the street that took me to my office. The snow was blowing so hard that I did not see the snow bank. The car didn't make it through. Now my car was suspended in midair on a mound of snow and would not go anywhere. The wheels spun. Rocking the car forward and backward did no good. I was stuck. Fortunately workers from the church construction project came and helped pull my car out of the snow. What concerned me later was that the wind chill was nearing 50°F below zero and I still had to travel home. Fear came over me. With my string of luck, I knew that something awful lay ahead. I didn't want to go out in the cold. I didn't want to drive my car. If someone had come by and offered me a ride, I would have taken them up on it. I was wondering to myself, *What did I do to merit such abuse?*

To say that Shadrach, Meshach and Abednego faced a test would be an understatement. My bad week and the misfortune of Duddy, Hosking and Benson don't hold a candle to what these three men went through. Upon refusing to bow down to the idol that King Nebuchadnezzar had made, they were bound and thrown into a blazing furnace that had been heated to maximum intensity. Why did such a calamity come upon them? Had they done wrong? Had they committed a heinous crime? No. Their only fault was that they listened to God rather than to the king. Their crisis was one of faithfulness—standing for what they believed. They were serious God followers who would not worship or serve anything or anyone but almighty God. Their response provides insight and wisdom when life gets too hot because we, too, are faithful.

Advance Decision Making

The phone rang in the middle of the night at a pastor's home. The house of a young couple who were members of his church was on fire and burning to the ground. The pastor traveled to the home. The street was blocked with emergency vehicles, fire trucks, news camera crews and floodlights. As the pastor walked toward the house, someone informed him that it was too late. The husband had rushed back into the house to rescue their new baby and had never returned. The pastor learned that the wife had been taken to the hospital emergency room. As the pastor drove to the hospital, he had no idea what to do or what to say. Here was a young woman who had lost everything.

What could he say?

When he found her, she was sitting in an area with drawn curtains, her face covered with soot. Before he could say anything, she looked up at him and said, "Pastor, the Lord is the strength of my life."

This young woman did not decide at that moment to view life in that way. Obviously it had been her practice for years to say, "The Lord is the strength of my life." And to mean it. When she most needed that strength, it was there.

Likewise, when Shadrach, Meshach and Abednego were faced with the choice of bowing down to a heathen idol or of remaining loyal to their God, the decision had already been made. Earlier in their life they had made the nonnegotiable resolution that they would serve God no matter what. No matter where they were, at home or in a distant land. No matter who they were with, friends or enemies. No matter when they were challenged, young or old. Their conviction had been made. Everyone may have been falling down to worship this statue, but not them.

Before we are thrust into the fiery furnace, it's imperative that we decide in advance to remain faithful to God. The question is not *if* the hot times will come but *when.* They will blow upon us like a tornado on the Midwestern plains, forcefully and unexpectedly. Convictions forged in advance will keep us strong. Failing to decide, we will be like a leaf in the raging tornado, tossed and blown at the whim of the storm. In our case we will be at the mercy of the people and the circumstances surrounding our crises. Sealing our conviction that we remain faithful and loyal to God no matter what helps us ride out the storm.

> **The question is not *if* the hot times will come but *when.***

Our Tests Test God

When we are thrown into the fiery furnace, God's reputation is as much at stake as ours. God has promised to be with us, to protect us, to shield us and to make a way for us through the difficulties of life. He has never promised that he will prevent the tests from coming our way, but he has declared that he will see us through them.

Why did Nebuchadnezzar bind the three Hebrews before throwing them in the furnace? Why did Nebuchadnezzar increase the temperature to maximum intensity? Why did Nebuchadnezzar have his strongest soldiers escort the Hebrew boys to the furnace? The answer is found in Nebuchadnezzar's statement "What god will be able to rescue you from my hand?" (Daniel 3:15). Nebuchadnezzar was afraid of God. And he should have been. These three Hebrews exhibited by their actions that they feared their God more than they feared Nebuchadnezzar's furnace.

When Nebuchadnezzar threw Shadrach, Meshach and Abednego into the fiery furnace, he was throwing down the gauntlet before God. The test that Shadrach, Meshach and Abednego faced, God now faced. Nebuchadnezzar essentially was issuing a challenge to God. He drew a line in the sand and dared God to cross over.

And God did.

This drama reveals that when we face tests and challenges and furnaces, God faces them too. His reputation is on the line. His name is being challenged. His power is being called into question.

Therefore we give our tests to God. And when we do, it reveals another observation.

God's Ways Are Different from Ours

Once, the lone survivor of a shipwreck was marooned on an uninhabited island. He managed to build a hut in which he put everything he had saved from the wreck. He prayed to God for rescue and anxiously scanned the horizon every day to signal any passing ship.

One day he returned to his hut from the beach, and to his horror he found the hut in flames and all of his possessions gone. What a tragedy! He sat down and cried. He shook his fist at God and said, "Why did I pray for your help? You have just brought disaster." But shortly thereafter a ship arrived. "We saw your smoke signal and hurried here," the captain explained. The shipwrecked man fell to his knees to thank God for the fire that had caused his rescue.

Can't you just hear the three teenagers talking to each other as they are escorted before Nebuchadnezzar's throne? "God is going to save us. How do you think he's going to do it?"

Shadrach says, "I think God will change the heart of the king. That old man likes us. He won't hurt us. Why, he has too much invested in us."

"You have it all wrong," Meshach interjects. "God will be more dramatic than that. He will send a plague like in Moses' day. Or he will send a fire from heaven like with Elijah on Mount Carmel. The king thinks he knows fire, but he's playing with the one who created it."

"No, no, no," Abednego chimes in. "God will snatch us away at the last moment. When we are thrown into the furnace, an angel will intercept us and deliver us from harm."

When the Hebrews go before Nebuchadnezzar, the king shows his favor to the youths. "Boys, you know I like you. So I'm giving you a second chance. Either turn from the worship of your God or else burn in my furnace."

"See," Shadrach says, "God's working on him."

The boys refuse to bow a second time. This ticks off the king. He orders the temperature raised and the boys bound. "There's going to be a barbecue," the king smirks.

"We've got nothing to sweat," says Meshach as they are being bound by the soldiers. "This is just like with Elijah. Instead of water, it is ropes. Instead of an altar, it is a furnace. God's going to save us before we get to the furnace. Just wait, you'll see."

As they are hobbling toward the furnace, Abednego is heard to say, "Okay, God, where's the angel? Anytime now, God. It's getting hotter!"

Shadrach, Meshach and Abednego, not unlike us, thought they had God all figured out. They didn't question God's power to rescue them; they simply thought they could establish God's agenda on when, where and how he would perform the miracle. They learned an important lesson: God's ways are not our ways. The Lord said through Isaiah the prophet,

> My thoughts are not your thoughts,
>   neither are your ways my ways. . . .
> As the heavens are higher than the earth,
>   so are my ways higher than your ways
>   and my thoughts than your thoughts. (Isaiah 55:8-9)

The God of the universe has a plan for the world and our lives and he is busy putting it into practice in his time and in his way. For us, his thoughts and ways are not easy to discern. They are often above and beyond us.

We would do well to learn that God works in ways we haven't thought of as we face life's fiery furnaces. And when we learn this lesson, it makes clear the next observation.

God Cannot Be Seen Until . . .

The three young Hebrews were looking for God. They looked for him when they refused to bow before the statue, but he was not seen. They looked for him as they stood in the presence of Nebuchadnezzar, but he was not noticed. They looked for God as they were being taken captive to the furnace, but he was not perceived. For these three faithful God followers, God was not visible until they were in the furnace.

In the furnace a fourth being appeared.

Can you imagine the surprise of Shadrach, Meshach and Abednego? In the midst of their crisis, thinking death was imminent, they looked up and saw God. Thinking they had figured out God's plan and God's timing,

> God was seen not only *from* the flames but also *in* the flames.

they realized that God could work when the door was locked and the flames the hottest. This mission impossible became a mission possible. What did they see? They looked into the face of God—and God smiled.

Nebuchadnezzar was surprised. He, too, saw God. "Weren't there three men that we tied up and threw into the fire? . . . Look! I see four men walking around in the fire, unbound and unharmed, and the fourth looks like a son of the gods" (Daniel 3:24-25). Nebuchadnezzar looked into the furnace and, upon seeing the fourth man, he too was amazed. He had witnessed a miracle.

God was seen, not only *from* the flames but also *in* the flames. Consider it a reminder that, if we want to see God, we should look for him when life gets hot.

Granted, we should never wish for the fiery furnaces of life. But when the flames of misfortune leap in our faces, we need to know with total assurance that, if we look for God, he is visible. During the difficult times, God reveals himself to us. If only we look for him.

Robert Louis Stevenson's father was an engineer who built lighthouses on the coasts of England and Scotland. One day he took Robert with him on an inspection trip. Near Bell Rock, off the Irish coast, their ship was struck by a gale that lasted more than twenty-five hours and terrified young Robert. His father went on deck, where only the captain stood. The captain had bound himself with a rope to the foremast to keep from being washed overboard. After approaching the captain, Stevenson returned to their cabin below. "Will the ship break up and sink, Father? And will we all drown?" asked young Robert.

"No," said his father in calm assurance. "We will out ride the storm. I looked into the pilot's face and he smiled."

Like Shadrach, Meshach and Abednego, when we face the trials and storms of life, we too need to look into our heavenly Father's face. And behind a frowning providence we will see a smiling face.

The fire not only reveals something about God; it reveals something about us too. That is the next observation.

Our Faith

God was true to his word. He promised that when believers go through fiery trials he would be with them. The three Hebrew teenagers experienced, quite literally, this promise:

> When you walk through the fire,
>   you will not be burned;
>   the flames will not set you ablaze. (Isaiah 43:2)

They must have read Job's story. Job said of God, "When he has tested me [in the fire], I will come forth as gold" (Job 23:10).

The fire reveals the authenticity of our faith. Just as the iron ore goes through the refining fire and comes out pure, so too does our faith. Actually, there may be something questionable about a faith that never walks through the fire. An army going through basic training is not yet ready for battle. Not until soldiers face the battle and have been under fire do they consider themselves proven, hardened, worthy. A ship's builder cannot prove that the vessel is sturdily built as long as it stays in dry dock. Its hull must get wet; it must endure a storm to demonstrate genuine seaworthiness. The same is true of our faith. When we hold fast to belief in Christ in spite of the fiery-furnace experiences of life, then we demonstrate the genuineness of our faith.

This was the case with Shadrach, Meshach and Abednego. When they were about to be cast into the fiery furnace, they said, "If we are thrown into the blazing furnace, the God we serve is able to save us from it, and he will rescue us from your hand, O king. But even if he does not, we want you to know, O king, that we will not serve your gods or worship the image of gold you have set up" (Daniel 3:17-18). They expected a miracle, but if it did not come, it would not shake their faith in God. Their faith didn't require a miracle. They would be true to God without it.

This was their defining moment.

Advancement Follows Adversity

The three Hebrews made their choice, stood the test, saw the face of God, proved their faith genuine. Now they were in line for a promotion. "Then the king promoted Shadrach, Meshach and Abednego in the province of Babylon" (Daniel 3:30). Isn't it interesting, as with Joseph and Mordecai and Nehemiah, how God employed pagans to promote God followers who demonstrated by their choices, convictions and character where their allegiance lay?

> Pain always precedes promotion.

What the three boys encountered reveals an important spiritual truth: advancement follows adversity. What is true in athletics and academics is also true in spiritual matters. Pain always precedes promotion. I would like to say that it isn't so, but it is.

The apostle Paul understood the truth of this spiritual principle when he wrote, "Our light and momentary troubles are achieving for us an eternal glory that far outweighs them all" (2 Corinthians 4:17). The fires of life and the troubles of a fallen world are part of the process of working out our future glory. No pain, no gain. No adversity, no advancement.

A man who handcrafted violins focused on the kind of wood that made the best violin. He used fine domestic woods. He imported excellent foreign woods. He used aging processes to harden the woods. Yet in all of this the tone he desired from his violins remained beyond his reach.

One day he found a gnarled piece of wood that came from the timberline, that zone where trees stop growing on a mountainside. The blasts of winter storms, the slashing rain and the wind-swept bleakness of a mountaintop had twisted the wood and hardened it. Yet the violin created from that wood taken at timberline produced a heavenly tone unlike anything else ever made.

Some of us live at the timberline, facing the trials and troubles of this painful world. But there is where God puts the music in our lives.

Ordinary coal in the bowels of the earth is placed under pressure of 1.5 million pounds per square inch at a temperature of 5000°F. Out of that heat and pressure the beauty of a diamond is born. We too have the raw materials within us to reflect the glory of God, to sing the music of the gospel and to advance beyond our adversity. Those raw materials can become radiant with splendor when we undergo the heat and pressure of the fiery furnaces of life. And live to tell about it.

Charles Spurgeon, the famed British preacher of the nineteenth century, preached out of the furnace of intense personal suffering from gout and related diseases. Furthermore his wife was an invalid confined to her room during the ten most productive years of his ministry. As the preacher sat in her room one evening, a log whistled in the fireplace. Gases trapped in the wood were released, causing a brief, musical tone. Spurgeon told his wife, Susannah, "It takes the fire to bring out the music."

What is true of logs is true of life.

Michael Benson, Craig Hosking and Chris Duddy learned that truth. So did Shadrach, Meshach and Abednego. And so can we.

Study Questions

1. Describe an event in which you thought you were going to die.

2. Have you ever been punished because of your faithfulness? How did it feel?

3. What are some convictions that you will stand for no matter what?

4. What does this statement mean: "Your tests test God"?

5. Identify a situation in which the event you thought was a disaster actually turned out to be a blessing.

6. In what ways have you witnessed the presence of God in the midst of great tragedy or difficulty?

7. How does your positive reaction to crises demonstrate the genuineness of your faith?

8. How has the principle that advancement follows adversity been evident in your life?

Six

When Your Integrity Is Tested

*I*n his thirteen-year career with the Minnesota Twins, Kirby Puckett won the hearts of children and adults alike. He hit .318 for his career, made the All-Star lineup ten years in a row and won six Gold Gloves for defensive play in center field. He twice led his team to World Series championships. But what really made Kirby stand out was the integrity he displayed.

Kirby was generous, giving away millions in free tickets, scholarships, medical treatment and community service. He worked hard every day, showing up early year after year, training diligently rather than just depending on enormous talent and ego to play the game. He was steady, doing his best every game, whether the Twins were first or last in the standings. He was one of the few professional athletes to turn down a better contract elsewhere in order to stay with his team and keep his family from having to move.

But for Kirby Puckett 1996 was a bad year. Glaucoma had irreversibly damaged his right eye. He could no longer see well enough to play.

On Saturday, September 9, 1996, Twins fans paid tribute to Kirby Puckett at the Metrodome. Thousands stood outside, while inside 51,000 fans, friends and journalists wept as he entered the field to say goodbye for the last time. He thanked them and told them not to worry, life was not over. As Kirby left the Metrodome, slowly driving around the field with his wife, Tonya, beside him, a beaming little kid leaned over the edge of the left field wall and jiggled a jersey with Kirby's number on it: thirty-four. Kirby saluted him, and as he disappeared from view, so too did the kid's smile. Then the kid laid his head on the top of the ledge and began to cry.

Kirby is missed, but he's remembered as a man of integrity.

What Is Integrity?

Integrity is to personal character what health is to the body or 20/20 vision is to the eyes. A person of integrity is whole; his or her life is put together. In other words, who that person is when people are watching is the same as who that person is when no one is watching.

> Our integrity is the internal script that determines our response to failure, mistreatment and pain.

Integrity is who we truly are. It will affect how much we accomplish. It will determine whether or not we are worth knowing. As with the little kid in the stands when Kirby Puckett left the stadium, it will determine whether people will cry when we leave, be it a game or a team or a business or a church or the world.

Our integrity is the internal script that determines our response to failure, mistreatment and pain. Integrity enabled Kirby Puckett to say, "Don't worry; life is not over." Integrity also determines our response to success (perhaps the greatest test of integrity). Stretched out in a locker room, Kirby Puckett once said, "You don't know how long God wants you here, so you should always give all thanks to him."[1]

Integrity reaches into every room of our lives. It is more far-reaching than our talent, our education, our background or our network of friends. Integrity is a lot like water; it seeps into and out of all the cracks of our lives. And when integrity is lost . . . well, hear the words of an anonymous author who penned, "When wealth is lost, nothing is lost; when health is lost, something is lost; when character is lost, all is lost."

Suffice it to say that integrity is more about who we are (our being) than what we accomplish (our doing). It has to do with intangibles. Objective yardsticks and impressive awards can't measure the kind of people we become deep down inside. Of the two, *being* will ultimately outdistance *doing* every time. It may take half a lifetime to perfect, but hands down, it's far more valuable. And lasting. And inspiring.

I thank God for persons of being—persons of integrity like Kirby Puckett, and like the Old Testament character Daniel.

A Model of Integrity

Daniel is one of those biblical characters we usually associate with just one event. For Daniel, it is the lion's den. But instead we need to remember him because of the bottom-line message of his life: his integrity. It seeped out of every pore of his life. It was the reason he was thrown in the lion's den in the first place.

The story of Daniel, like the story of Kirby Puckett, communicates the message that sometimes life throws us a curve ball when we least expect it. And sometimes it shatters our face. Our integrity will determine how we respond.

This crisis was Daniel's defining moment.

Eleanor Roosevelt wrote, "You gain strength, courage and confidence by every experience in which you really stop to look fear in the face. You are able to say to yourself, 'I lived through this horror, I can take the next thing that comes along.' . . . You must do the one thing you think you cannot do."[2] Daniel looked fear in the face and lived through the horror. From his experience, meeting life honestly and courageously, you and I can learn how to face the curve balls thrown at us. And in the end we will walk away with our integrity intact.

Integrity Distinguishes People

The king and all those who knew Daniel recognized his marks of distinction. "Now Daniel so distinguished himself among the administrators and the satraps by his exceptional qualities that the king planned to set him over the whole kingdom" (Daniel 6:3). Leadership distinguished Daniel.

He led with dignity, respecting the people under him. Daniel knew what John Maxwell wrote: "A charismatic personality will draw people; only integrity will keep them."[3] Or as Ralph Waldo Emerson said, "An institution is the lengthened shadow of one man."[4] Don't we want to be led by someone who keeps promises?

Daniel led with these attributes:

☐ Conduct—He was above reproach.

☐ Trustworthiness—He could be counted on.

☐ Morals—He lived a clean life.

☐ Faithfulness—He did his work.

☐ Consistency—His private life was compatible with his public image.

☐ Convictions—He willingly followed God even at personal cost.

People like that stand above the rest of society like a giraffe towering over an antelope. Unfortunately, it seems like they are becoming endangered species.

James Kouzes and Barry Posner surveyed nearly fifteen hundred managers from around the country in a study sponsored by the American Management Association. They asked the following open-ended question: "What values, personal traits or characteristics do you look for and admire in your superiors?" More than 225 values, traits and characteristics were identified, and these were then reduced to fifteen categories. The most frequent response was "integrity, is truthful, is trustworthy, has character, has convictions."[5]

Daniel was a prototype of that kind of individual.

Integrity Is Tested

If we choose to be people of integrity, it will be put to the test every single day. Mark my words. At work we will be tempted to fudge on expense reports, to manipulate figures, to tell lies to get a sale or to compromise our convictions. At school we will be tempted to work off someone else's paper, to borrow last year's test or to pay for a research paper. On the road we will be tempted to watch an X-rated movie in the privacy of our hotel room or to take a few towels home. At home we will be tempted to break a promise to our children or to not fulfill a commitment to our spouse.

Several years ago a hopeful presidential candidate made a statement to the press. *The New York Times* quoted Senator Gary Hart from Colorado as saying, "Follow me around. I'm serious. If anyone wants to put a tail on me, go ahead." The news press did just that. When he was photographed with girlfriend Donna Rice, it meant the unraveling of a presidential candidacy.

In Daniel's time his enemies spied on him. They put his integrity to the test. They searched through his personal effects. "The administrators and the satraps tried to find grounds for charges against Daniel in his conduct of government affairs, but they were unable to do so. They could find no corruption in him, because he was trustworthy and neither corrupt nor negligent" (Daniel 6:4). Daniel was put to the test and he passed.

People of integrity have nothing to hide and nothing to fear. As the proverb says, "The man of integrity walks securely" (Proverbs 10:9).

Integrity Draws Fire

A person of integrity is like an oak tree. Strong. Tall. Deeply rooted. Growing upward. Fruitful. And, yes, exposed to life's storms. In a thunderstorm, which tree is most likely to draw the lightning strike? Lightning, more times than not, strikes the tallest object. Consequently, we can expect that those who stand tallest for God will draw fire.

Case in point: Daniel. "So the king gave the order, and they brought Daniel and threw him into the lions' den" (Daniel 6:16). Daniel was not in the lions' den because he had done something wrong but because he had done something right. That's a little confusing, isn't it? We are under the impression that, when we do what is wrong, we will be punished for it and that, when we do what is right, we will be rewarded for it. That makes good sense—but it isn't always true. Sometimes, when we do things wrong, we are rewarded for it (as far as this world is concerned), and occasionally, when we do what is right, we pay a terrible price for it.

> Those who stand tallest for God will draw fire.

A few years ago my friend Karen faced a real dilemma. Karen, part of a management team at work, is responsible for cost and schedule management. "In other words," she explains, "it's my job to make sure my company delivers whatever we're developing to our client on schedule and for the price specified in our contract." Working with the space station program, Karen realized a few years into the contract that her company would not be able to deliver what was promised. She went to her superiors.

They told her to massage the figures. "Make it work."

"But I can't do that," she said. "It wouldn't be right."

"Either do it or we will find someone else who will do it."

Karen wrestled with her decision over the weekend. She was in a real lions'-den predicament. What would she do? On Monday she faced the threat of losing her job because of doing what was right. As a matter of fact, on Monday she was fired.

Professional golfer Tom Watson at an early age had his heart set on being a champion. He also had his personal code of honor firmly in mind. In the first state tournament that he ever entered, he put his putter down behind the ball on one of the greens. To his dismay, the ball moved slightly. No one saw it. Of that he was certain. He was under great pressure to win, and there was no time to add up the pluses and minuses of the alternatives. But he knew without hesitation what he must do. He went over to an official and said, "My ball moved." That action cost him a stroke, and he lost the hole. Tom Watson placed his personal integrity ahead of his keen desire to win.

Tim, a recent high-school graduate, learned early in his adult life that being a Christian and being a friend can pose some unsettling dilemmas. Last summer he accepted an invitation to spend the night with some high-school buddies. Early in the evening the group decided to go to a nearby nightclub. The idea sent shock waves through Tim's value system, yet telling his friends he wouldn't go was painful. Tim said no and it cost him his pride and his friends.

Daniel was not the last man to suffer for doing what was right. It cost him to keep his integrity intact. Likewise, Kirby suffered. Karen suffered. Tom suffered. Tim suffered. And we will suffer.

Count on it. Integrity always draws fire.

Integrity Reflects the Character of God

Biblical integrity finds its source in the nature of God rather than in the behavioral patterns of people. Biblical integrity is a reflection of the character of God. Our heavenly Father and his Son are integrity personified. They are not simply pictures of the real thing. They *are* the real thing.

As Daniel demonstrated integrity, he was merely reflecting the image of God. As a friend of mine says, "We, like the moon, have no light, no energy, no power. Yet we, like the moon, when touched by the Son, cast his brilliance on the blackest of nights."

A judge was campaigning for reelection. He had a reputation for integrity. He was a distinguished and honorable gentleman of no small charity. Yet his opponent was conducting a vicious, mud-smearing, unfair campaign against him.

Somebody approached the judge, asking, "Do you know what your opponent is saying about you? Do you know he is criticizing you? How are you going to handle it? What are you going to do about it?"

The judge looked at his counselors and his campaign committee and calmly replied, "Well, when I was a boy, I had a dog. And every time the moon was full that hound dog would howl and bark at the bright face of the moon. We never did sleep well those nights. He would bark and howl at the moon all night."

"That's beside the point," his campaign manager said impatiently. "You've told us a nice story about your dog, but what are you going to do about your critic?"

The judge explained, "I just answered you! When the dog barked at the moon, the moon kept right on shining! I don't intend to do anything but keep right on shining. And I'll ignore the criticism, as the moon ignored the dog. I'll just keep right on shining! Quietly, calmly, beautifully."

That's what Daniel did. His enemies conspired. The lions roared. But he kept right on shining—quietly, calmly and beautifully.

The world is dark and needs the brightness of our integrity. Will we let it shine?

How Is Integrity Developed?

Three actions in the life of Daniel made him shine brightly. These same three actions need to be implemented in our lives if we are to display character. And by the way, they need to be practiced *before* the lion's-den experiences of our lives. Robert Freeman said, "Character is not made in a crisis—it is only exhibited."[6] If we wait till the moment of testing, it is too late.

Consistently pray to God. "Three times a day he got down on his knees and prayed, giving thanks to his God, just as he had done before" (Daniel 6:10). Daniel didn't turn to prayer in a panic. He had made prayer a regular habit of his life. Prayer was his first priority, not his last resort.

Continually serve God. "The king said to Daniel, 'May your God, whom you serve continually, rescue you!' " (Daniel 6:16). Peter T. Forsythe was right when he said, "The first duty of every soul is to find not its freedom but its Master."[7] Once we find our Master, Jesus Christ, we will find our freedom. Nobody can successfully serve two masters. To attempt to do so is to become a fractional person, and a fractional person doesn't have integrity. Daniel would not serve two masters. He would not compromise his convictions.

Conscientiously trust in God. "When Daniel was lifted from the den, no wound was found on him, because he had trusted in his God" (Daniel 6:23). Regardless of the outcome, Daniel was going to trust God. That takes courage and conviction, but it results in integrity. It is the ability to choose faithfulness and resist compromise. He chose to trust God regardless of the outcome. He was willing to lose his place and his friends and his status because he would trust God no matter what.

Remember the little boy who laid his head down and cried when Kirby Puckett left the stadium? Kirby Puckett had a visible effect on that young man. Remember what happened to the king after he sealed the den of lions with Daniel on the inside? "Then the king returned to his palace and spent the night without eating and without sleeping and without any entertainment being brought to him. And he could not sleep" (Daniel 6:18). Daniel had a visible effect on the king. Here's the point. Men and women of integrity distinguish themselves by their whole and sincere lives. People take notice of lives lived with distinction.

One of my favorite movies is *To Kill a Mockingbird,* starring Gregory

Peck as Atticus Finch, an Alabama lawyer defending a black man accused of raping a white girl in the early 1930s. Upon taking the case, Finch immediately comes under the abuse and scorn of the people in the town. The man was innocent and Atticus Finch defended him capably; but when the jury came in, nobody was surprised that its verdict was guilty.

The lawyer's two children were at the courthouse. Unable to find seats downstairs, they had gone into the segregated balcony and had sat next to the town's black preacher. As the judge retired and the spectators filed out of the courtroom, Jean, Atticus's daughter, was engrossed in watching her father. He stood alone in the room, transferring papers from the table into his briefcase. Then he put on his coat and walked down the middle aisle toward the exit—a beaten man but a man with his soul intact. Jean felt someone touch her shoulder. She turned around and noticed that everyone in the balcony was standing. The black preacher nudged her again and said, "Miss Jean Louise, stand up. Your father's passin' by."

Those people were visibly moved by one man's integrity. Likewise, people may trick us, deceive us, test us, ignore us and criticize us. But know and understand this: one day they will stand up when we pass by because we faced life's curve balls with integrity.

Study Questions

1. Who are the people in your life who display integrity? How are they different from others?

2. What does the following statement mean to you: "When wealth is lost, nothing is lost; when health is lost, something is lost; when character is lost, all is lost"?

3. When your integrity was put to the test, what did you learn from those experiences?

4. How did you feel when you were punished for doing the right thing?

5. How can a believer reflect the light of Christ in testing situations?

6. Three actions in the life of Daniel enabled him to stand the test. He consistently prayed to God. He continually served God. He conscientiously trusted in God. How are you functioning in each of those areas?

7. What are the three distinguishing characteristics of your life?

Seven

When You
Are Treated Unfairly

I remember the day as though it were yesterday. I raced into the house, slammed the door behind me and started gushing tears like a waterfall. My wife attempted to make sense out of this unexpected display of emotion. "What's wrong?" she asked in desperation.

Three hours earlier I had left for graduate school confident and ready to defend my master's thesis. The past year had produced an emotional and physical drain of researching, writing, editing and preparing for the two-hour ordeal. But the school's administration had informed me that entrance into the Ph.D. program was certain if I completed the master's work. I had driven myself toward that coveted degree for years. So, to the best of my ability, I answered and defended my conclusions for my professors.

Following the thesis defense, I left the room so that the professors could discuss my performance in private. When I returned, they informed me that I had passed. My heart leaped with joy at having reached this milestone, but it was about to fall to the floor. "Good job," remarked the supervisory professor, "but the graduate committee has rejected your application into the doctoral program. We wanted to tell you personally before the rejection letter arrived in the mail." My professors explained the school's reasoning as I tried to keep back the onrush of tears.

I managed to hold the tears in check until I returned home. But once there, I cried uncontrollably. "It isn't fair," I snuffled through the sobs. "The school's administration led me to believe that I would be admitted to the doctoral program if I completed the master's. It isn't fair."

For the three years leading up to this moment my wife and I had planned and saved and given up so much for this lifelong dream of mine. Now the dream was crushed on the rocks of disappointment. Could anything good come out of this experience?

Many times I had counseled people with the three words "Life isn't fair." Now I swallowed them myself. They went down hard and bitter.

Bad things do happen to people. Schedules do not go as planned. Businesses go bankrupt. Employees are laid off. Athletic contests are lost. Scholarships are given to others. Relationships are broken. Unfortunately no one is exempt from such raw deals. Augustine was right: "God had one son on earth without sin, but never one without suffering."[1]

The dilemma that confronts us when injustice prevails is knowing whether the event is good or bad for us. An immediate evaluation is not always accurate. Many times what appears as a misfortune may turn out to be a great opportunity. When will the good happen? How will it happen? I do not know. I just know that God in his sovereignty has the way and the will to transform adversity, misfortune and heartache into something beautiful.

A Classic Example

The story of the Old Testament character Joseph is a classic account of life being unfair.

Joseph was reared in a large home, the second to last of eleven brothers. He was loved by his father but hated by his brothers. Their hate was so vengeful that they sought to kill him. When they got the chance, they threw him in a pit. Shortly thereafter a caravan came along and the brothers decided to sell him as a slave.

Talk about unfairness. My experience in graduate school seems insignificant in comparison.

Joseph was carried off to Egypt and sold to a man named Potiphar. While managing Potiphar's estate with distinction, Joseph was the object of an attempted seduction by Potiphar's wife. Since he refused to go to bed with her, she got revenge by claiming that he had tried to rape her.

And thus Joseph was thrown in prison. But as in Potiphar's household, in prison Joseph displayed his tremendous leadership ability. The warden placed Joseph in charge of all the inmates.

Two of Pharaoh's assistants, the baker and the cupbearer, were also imprisoned. While in prison, they had dreams that troubled them. Joseph correctly interpreted these dreams—the baker was going to die, but the cupbearer was going to be restored to his previous position. All Joseph asked in return for telling the cupbearer the interpretation was that, if he got the chance, he would mention Joseph to Pharaoh so that Joseph, too, could leave prison. But when the cupbearer was released from prison and returned to work for Pharaoh, he forgot Joseph.

Two years passed. Then one night Pharaoh had a dream, which no one was able to interpret. Finally the cupbearer remembered Joseph. At the cupbearer's recommendation, Pharaoh summoned Joseph. He came to the palace and interpreted Pharaoh's dream to mean that Egypt would experience seven years of bountiful harvest followed by seven years of famine. Since Pharaoh believed that Joseph had interpreted his dream correctly, Joseph was placed in charge of the palace and the whole land of Egypt to prepare for this crisis.

Joseph went from a prison to a palace.

The Common Thread

Taking a bad situation and making something good out of it is not uncommon. More than one person affirms, "I have no problems in life; I only have opportunities." The pages of history books are filled with stories of individuals who encountered setbacks, only to make something positive out of them. They were the better for it. And in many cases so are we.

Thomas Edison, when a boy, received a blow on his ear that impaired his hearing. But later he believed his deafness was a blessing, for it was the means by which he was saved from distractions. This allowed him to concentrate on his work, and out of that concentration emerged some of the greatest inventions of all time.

Victor Hugo, a literary genius of France, was exiled from his country by Napoleon. But out of that period of exile arose some of his most creative works. When he later returned home in triumph, he asked, "Why was I not exiled earlier?"

Helen Keller, born blind and deaf, faced obstacle after obstacle in her life. However, on more that one occasion she confided, "I thank God for my obstacles, for through them I have found myself, my work and my God."

George Frederick Handel was at a low point in his life. His money was gone and his creditors hounded him, threatening him with imprisonment. His right side became paralyzed and his health deteriorated. For a brief time he was tempted to give up. In the midst of the darkness he picked himself up and began to do the only thing he knew to do—write music. And out of that despair he wrote the oratorio known as *Messiah*, which many consider the greatest piece of church music in history.

The fiber tying Edison, Hugo, Keller and Handel together is that these people refused to be defeated by their problems. They saw their misfortunes not as calamities to destroy them but as opportunities to grow and develop in ways that otherwise would have been impossible.

That was Joseph's strength too. Joseph succeeded in spite of his unfair circumstances. He responded to difficult crises with a positive attitude. He developed a godly character in the midst of unjust suffering. He discovered in his defining moment that when life is unfair God is still good.

I do not know when he learned this truth, but he did learn it. His life and attitude can be summarized by his own words to his brothers: "You intended to harm me, but God intended it for good to accomplish what is now being done, the saving of many lives" (Genesis 50:20).

Focus on God

When things go wrong, we often focus on self rather than God. That is, we reject the one whom we need the most. God loves to take people from prisons to palaces, to turn slaves into sons. He has a lot of practice—he turned a crucifixion into a resurrection.

How do we focus on God?

First, we focus on God by remembering his presence. "The LORD was with Joseph and he prospered" (Genesis 39:2). Five times the Scriptures say that God was with Joseph. It would be well for us, when faced with unfair predicaments and unjust suffering, to remember that we are not alone. God is there and he cares.

Second, we focus on God by recalling God's promises. God had promised Joseph that he would be a leader, that his life would count. Joseph clung to that promise even in the worst of situations. God has promises for us too. All of the promises recorded in Scripture are like a blank check with God's signature on it, just waiting for us to cash it in.

Third, we focus on God by realizing God's purpose. The climax of the story of Joseph occurred when his father died and the brothers were afraid that Joseph would bring harm to them for their dastardly and spiteful act. Joseph assured them that God had a good reason for his being sold into slavery. Because of his slavery and imprisonment, the lives of many people were spared, including those of his family. Often when suffering accosts our lives we ask God, "Why is this happening?" We should instead ask God, "What can I learn?" Pain has a hidden purpose. Our lives are redirected through failure. When we seek God's purpose, those crises become clear in time.

As the night of my rejection by the graduate committee turned to dawn, I began to glimpse the truth that, while life is unjust, God is fair and he can be trusted. He is a good God who has a plan for my life. He is sovereign, and his sovereignty is laced with love. It took a heartbreaking experience for me to realize this wonderful truth. As I faced the dark days of my disappointment, I began to focus on God. I claimed the Lord's right to lead my life. I accepted the truth that he knew what was best for me.

> Pain has a hidden purpose.

Focusing on God did not mean I would not experience pain. I did. But in the midst of my pain I believed that God was at work for my ultimate good. I could accept adversity by choosing to claim that God's goodness would prevail. God's ultimate goal for my life was, and is, not my comfort but the conformity of my life to his Son's.

The months that followed my disappointment were unstable. Much of my life was tossed up in the air. What would we do? Where would we go? Through it all, though, I trusted in the presence, the promises and the purpose of God. I was experiencing the words of the New Testament writer firsthand,

> Never will I leave you;
>> never will I forsake you. (Hebrews 13:5)

I walked away from my experience as Joseph walked away from his, knowing that when I faced difficulty, suffering and unfairness, God was there. He could be counted on.

Forget the Past

"The world has trapped us with a deceiving belief: We are products of our environment and experience," wrote Robert S. McGee in *Search for Significance*. "We are the sum of our past performances and failures, with little or no hope of raising ourselves to any greater sense of accomplishment."[2] Consequently, many people are defeated by their past. They live as victims of their past.

I read an interesting word derivation. Sabots were the crude wooden shoes worn by French workers. Whenever factory owners excessively abused these workers, they would retaliate by throwing their sabots into the machinery—hence *sabot*aging it. Sabotage stopped the works.

We sabotage our lives just as surely by throwing into our mind messages of negativism and painful memories of the past. Such thoughts will jam us up so that we cannot grow and live victoriously.

It doesn't have to be that way.

When Joseph came to lead Pharaoh's palace, he married and had children. "Joseph named his firstborn Manasseh and said, 'It is because God has made me forget all my troubles and all my father's household' " (Genesis 41:51). The root of the name Manasseh means "to forget." But in the Hebrew construction of this word, Manasseh means "to take the sting out of the memory." Joseph had many painful memories from a troubled past.

One of the most remarkable aspects of Joseph's life was that he did not wallow in self-pity or harbor bitterness or seek revenge. God removed the sting of injustice.

We cannot change the past; we can only heal the hurt that comes to us from the past. People wrestling with painful memories need a healing of the memories or a "holy amnesia" to the misfortune and suffering of their past. Bad memories need not defeat us. They can be replaced with positive and true thoughts. Joseph could have been a bitter and resentful man because of his past; he chose instead to be a forgiving and hopeful man. So can we if we allow God to do his work in our minds.

Fruitful in Work

"The second son he named Ephraim and said, 'It is because God has made me fruitful in the land of my suffering' " (Genesis 41:52). Joseph was like cream that rises to the top. Whenever he faced troubles and was placed in difficult situations, he did not allow adversity to defeat him. In each incident, whether it was as a slave or in prison or in the royal palace of Egypt, he was made responsible for all the affairs. How easy it would have been to rationalize mistreatment and tread water in inactivity. But not Joseph. He fulfilled his responsibilities and consequently was fruitful in his work.

One of the greatest Christian witnesses is the performance of our work. Even though we may not enjoy our labor, even though we may be passed over for promotions, even though we may know that we can perform better than our superiors, yet we maintain a standard of excellence. We say, as Joseph must have said on many occasions, "I don't know why these things are happening to me, but I do know how to act."

The quality of our work reveals the quality of our spiritual life. Poor workmanship is a slam on God. It's not how we act on Sundays that demonstrates to the world our credibility as Christians; it's the way we behave on the job.

As Christians, we are called not to be better than others but simply to do our best. Abraham Lincoln wrote, "I do the very best I know how—the very best I can; and I mean to keep doing so until the end. If the end brings me out all right, what is said against me won't amount to anything. If the end brings me out wrong, ten angels swearing I was right would make no difference."[3]

Even in suffering and unfairness the traits of diligence, excellence and truthfulness should be our hallmarks.

Faithful in Character

Joseph was about as morally pure as any sinful human being could be. He was so clean that his detractors had to make up stuff about him. Even though he had every reason to blame God for his misfortunes and rationalize ungodly behavior, his character remained intact. When Potiphar's wife tried to seduce him, he would not succumb. "My master does not concern himself with anything in the house; everything he owns he has entrusted to my care. . . . How then could I do such a wicked thing and sin against God?" (Genesis 39:8-9). The motivation for Joseph's integrity was his loyalty to others and his love for God.

The basis for character is not determined by the majority of our peers or by the output of our glands but by the mandate of our Father in heaven. It's doing what we said we would do. It's keeping promises.

> The basis for character is not determined by the majority of our peers or by the output of our glands but by the mandate of our Father in heaven.

What we are trying to achieve is not nearly as important as who we are going to be. It's possible to perform many worthwhile activities and yet not be a person of authenticity. Unfortunately people emphasize doing rather than being, accomplishment rather than character. Many people are so wrapped up in making a living that they forget to make a life—a godly life.

Joseph's story reveals that character comes from within. It is not something we put on, create or buy. The character of God followers comes from the presence of God indwelling us. Like Joseph, we just have to let it shine through.

Forgive the Offender

The story of Joseph's life begins its climax with his brothers coming to

Egypt in search of food. Joseph had every reason to settle the score, to do great harm to these men. But he chose the higher road of forgiveness. Joseph told his brothers, "God sent me ahead of you to preserve for you a remnant on earth and to save your lives by a great deliverance" (Genesis 45:7).

Forgiveness seems unnatural and illogical. Our sense of fairness kicks in, telling us that people should pay for the wrongs they inflict. Following my rejection to the doctoral program, I talked with a successful businessman. His advice: "Get even. Do whatever it takes to make them pay." My anger agreed with his course of action. I also talked with a godly pastor. His counsel: "Forgive them and move on with your life. You'll be healthier and happier if you do." I wanted to seek revenge, but in time I chose to forgive. I discovered that forgiveness is love's power to break nature's rule of revenge. As I forgave I learned that forgiveness is love's toughest work and love's highest risk, but it provides life's richest rewards.

As I went through this experience, I recalled an event from the little lady of Holland, Corrie ten Boom. During World War II, Corrie and her sister were imprisoned in a concentration camp for harboring Jews escaping Hitler's terror. They were continually taken to the delousing shower and forced to strip naked. A lecherous SS guard ogled these very modest women during the whole humiliating time. Corrie survived the camp, but her sister did not.

After the war, Corrie became a Christian spokesperson all over the world, preaching forgiveness everywhere she went. One day she was speaking in Munich. At the end of the lecture a man came up to her and stuck out his hand, saying, "Ah yes, God's forgiveness is good, isn't it?" As she looked into his face, she recognized him as the lecherous SS guard. His face had been imprinted on her consciousness forever.

She recalled later, "I thought in my heart I had forgiven him, but as he reached his hand out, my hand froze by my side, and I could not reach out and take his hand. Here I was, the world-famous forgiver, and I had come face to face with a man I couldn't even touch. I prayed to God, 'God, forgive me for my inability to forgive.' When I asked God for that, he gave me the grace to reach out my hand, take that man's hand, and say, 'Yes, God is good.'"

Circumstances will change. And some of those circumstances will be bad. Our response to those circumstances, however, must not change. We must stay true to God's Word. In doing so, God will take the bad and make it good. He will take the broken pieces of our misfortune and shape them into a miracle. And when he does, it will be for us a defining moment.

The architects planning the royal palace in Tehran, Iran, ordered mirrors to cover the entrance walls. But when the mirrors arrived, it was found that they had all been broken in transit. There were thousands of pieces of smashed mirror. The builders were going to dispose of them all when one creative man said, "No, maybe it will be more beautiful because they are broken." He took some of the larger pieces and smashed them also and fitted them together like an abstract mosaic. When you see the result, it looks as though the domed ceiling and the side walls and the columns are all covered with diamonds. The edges of the myriad of little mirrors reflect the light, throwing out all the colors of the rainbow.

Broken to be made beautiful. That's what God wants to do in each of our lives. He did it for Joseph and he did it for me.

In my case, as the months dragged by, I slowly worked through the personal disappointment of not getting into the Ph.D. program. While I felt cheated and deceived by the administration for not being allowed into the program, I began to look at the situation a little differently.

During this time, some friends were visited by tragedy. The mother in the family was dying. The doctors knew it. The family knew it. But it wasn't fair! She was young and her family needed her.

As the family reflected on her life, they recognized God's undeserved graciousness. The family knew that nine years earlier she had been diagnosed with an inoperable malignant tumor and had not been expected to live for long. Now, in her last stand against death, I heard them say, "God has been good. He has given us nine more years, unexpected years, with her."

Considering that God had given me more than I deserved, I knew I should not think about what I was lacking. Instead I should rejoice in what I possessed. I had not been accepted into the Ph.D. program, but I still walked away from the school with a master's degree. I was better educated, qualified and equipped to perform my job than I had been before. Because of this setback, events unfolded that led me to my current position, which I've held since 1988. These years have been my most fruitful and fulfilling years in ministry, and in 1996 I walked across the stage to receive my doctorate from another institution.

Admittedly it was hard to keep from looking at what others had and what I lacked. All too frequently I had boiled life down to a comparison event. I kept checking out who had what degree or position or possession, then measuring it against what I had.

Through my experience I learned that life doesn't always deliver in equal portions for everyone. My problem is that I only see in the dimension of time, while God is weaving a tapestry out of my life with eternal purposes. I arrogantly presume that I am the best judge of fairness and equality. But I am not. God knows best. I simply need to trust him.

Study Questions

1. Describe a situation in your life in which something bad turned out to be good.

2. What do bad situations that turn out for good say about God?

3. What can you learn from the problems that are currently overwhelming you?

4. Pain often has a hidden purpose. What, in your opinion, is the hidden purpose in your painful situation?

5. What painful memories do you need to forget? Will you take a moment and ask God to help you deal with them and move past them?

6. Does your performance at work add to or detract from your witness for Christ? In what ways do you need to be a better employee?

7. What character traits do you want to be remembered for?

8. Who do you need to forgive, and why?

Eight

When You Encounter an Overwhelming Obstacle

*I*t shouldn't have happened.

In 1952 Hickory High School, with sixty-four students, defeated South Bend Central, with a student body of twenty-eight hundred, in the finals of the Indiana State High School Boys Basketball Tournament. It was a classic matchup. A small, rural school battled a large, city school. The road to the finals for little Hickory had been a rocky one. But in the finals they represented all the little guys everywhere. And in one shining moment they rose to the occasion. Their heroics made them state champions.

Giant killers.

The giants for Hickory High was the team put on the court by South Bend Central. The giants for us are those frustrating problems that stomp through our lives with fearful frequency. Sometimes they take the form of temptations from the devil. At other times they show up as conflicts with a person at work. Or any of a thousand monumental barriers that stand between us and a satisfying life.

How Do You Slay a Giant?

Since our early days in Sunday school, we have heard the story of David, the boy who slew a giant. He went to visit his brothers at the battlefront and discovered that they had a problem. A big one. His name was Goliath.

The army of Philistia, in which Goliath was a soldier, was at war with King Saul's army. The two armies faced each other across a large valley. They were of equal strength, and neither was willing to surrender the advantage of higher elevation to carry the battle to the enemy. To settle these kinds of stalemates, a peculiar custom ensued. Each side would choose a champion fighter, and the two would fight to the death. The army of the surviving champion was declared the winner.

Goliath was the Philistines' champion. He stood nine feet tall and was strong as a bull—and this was before steroids. The tip of his spear alone weighed fifteen pounds. For forty days he waved that ponderous spear like a toothpick, taunting the soldiers of Israel. "Are you men of Israel cowards?" he would roar. "Send someone out to fight me!"

Whether the Israelites were cowards is debatable. But they were not stupid—no one left their ranks to fight the giant!

David arrived at the height of the crisis, bringing food from home for his older brothers. He couldn't believe what he saw and heard. But mostly he couldn't believe what the men of Israel were doing about this giant-sized problem. They were having a committee meeting. They were just talking about what to do about this problem.

You know how the story ends. Little David, the shepherd boy, killed Goliath. In one shining moment he rose to the occasion and won the battle for all the little guys everywhere. You and me included.

It was his defining moment. For the balance of his life, regardless of all his other successes, David would be remembered as the youngster who slew a giant. And in doing so, he modeled for us how to slay the giants looming in our own lives.

Take the Battle to the Giant

The fictionalized movie *The Untouchables* shows how Elliott Ness, working for the U.S. Treasury Department, took down the crime boss Al Capone in Chicago during the days of Prohibition. Ness suffered setbacks and defeats in his pursuit to bring Capone to justice. The entire police force and city government stood in Ness's way to victory. It seemed that everyone was being paid off by the Capone organization. It seemed like a hopeless fight to bring down Chicago's crime leader. Finally Ness persuaded a crusty old Chicago policeman by the name of Malone, who was as honest as the day was long, to join forces with him. Throughout the story the old policeman mentors the young Ness.

In one pivotal scene Malone asks Ness, "Are you ready to go to work?" And then he hands out guns to the squad of four as they march out of the office.

"Where are we going?" asks Ness.

"On a liquor raid."

The group walks across the street to the post office. "What are we doing here?" Ness inquires.

"Liquor raid."

Ness looks around and then responds, "Here?"

Malone replies, "Mr. Ness, everybody knows where the booze is. The problem is not finding it. The problem is who wants to cross Capone."

When the federal officers break open the door, they see where rows and rows of barrels filled with booze are stored awaiting shipment.

We never have to wonder where the giants in our lives are. We know where they are. They are giants— you can't miss them. They are the habits and obstacles and hurdles that we can't escape. Everywhere we turn, they show up. To defeat them you have to take the battle to them.

> We never have to wonder where the giants in our lives are.

David had no problem identifying his giant. It was the bully Goliath, who was verbally abusing the Israelite army. All David had to do was walk out on the plain and fight the man.

There is a time for talking and there is a time for action. One husband said to his wife for the four-hundredth time after she asked him to do something, "I'm aiming to do that."

The wife replied, "Well, it's time to pull the trigger."

Few giants ever get talked to death. Thomas Carlyle wrote, "Do the duty which lies nearest thee, which thou knowest to be a duty! The second duty will already have become clearer."[1] Too often we spend our time fighting the battles we know we can win rather than fighting the giants that will require much effort. It's like tackling nonessential projects that are simple and easy while all the while you put off a massive, critically important project. While the giants loom, we ignore them to fight the foes that can be defeated easily.

Mike was a big talker. I don't think I ever met anyone who had such creative and grandiose dreams. Almost every week he would relate to me another fantastic plan. One week it was starting a printing business. Another week it was establishing a "Western Town" tourist attraction. Later it was a chain of custodial service outlets. Mike had great plans. He also had one big giant in his life: procrastination. Mike was all talk and no action. He had the "Someday I'll . . ." syndrome.

David's first principle of giant killing was to take action. He wasn't impulsive. He explored the problem and listened to advice from others. But then the time for talking ended. He offered his services to King Saul and took the battle to Goliath. He said, "Let no one lose heart on account of this Philistine; your servant will go and fight him" (1 Samuel 17:32). David took the battle to the giant. He knew that fighting easy battles would not eliminate the giant who loomed over the Israelites.

Realize That Prior Battles Have Prepared You to Fight the Present Giant

"Goliath, the Philistine champion from Gath, stepped out from his lines and shouted his usual defiance, and David heard it" (1 Samuel 17:23). The Philistines were not Israel's only enemy. There were the Ammonites, the Phoenicians and the Midianites. David could have volunteered for service on some distant front, to face some other giants rather than the feared one right in front of him. But Goliath was the giant causing immediate problems, so David said, "Let me take him on. I'll silence that bigmouth."

How could David be so confident? Simple. Goliath was not the first attacker David had brought down. David said to King Saul, "Your servant has killed both the lion and the bear; this uncircumcised Philistine will be like one of them" (1 Samuel 17:36). David had prepared himself by facing and gaining victory over smaller giants. Now he was ready to face a bigger test.

Giants will pop up throughout our lives. In the words of Kevin Costner in the movie *Field of Dreams*, "You build it and they will come." When we build our lives, the giants will come. It is a given. To shape a character pleasing to God, one must slay some giants. We therefore need to always be prepared, because we never know when they are going to show up. Abraham Lincoln, sixteenth president of the United States, faced and slew giant after giant in his life. He wrote to Governor Andrew Curtin of Pennsylvania, "I think the necessity of being ready increases.—Look to it."[2] That was the whole of his letter and the whole of his life. He lived ready for the callings that came his way. May the same be true for us.

Every four years Olympic hopefuls strive to earn gold, silver and bronze medals. The athletes will have spent a lifetime in training for perhaps just a few seconds in the arena, competing for a medal. A lifetime—really? Yes, a lifetime. Giant killing always requires a lifetime of preparation and training. In fact any worthy challenge is a lifetime undertaking. Along the way each small giant we overcome makes us stronger and more confident to defeat the next giant.

Attach Your Faith to a Great Big God

This text says as much about God as it does about David. It tells us that God wants us to defeat the giants in our lives. He does not want us to limp along through life as losers. Defeating giants comes from understanding who God is and what he can do for us.

Notice what David did. "He took his staff in his hand, chose five smooth stones from the stream, put them in the pouch of his shepherd's bag and, with his sling in his hand, approached the Philistine" (1 Samuel 17:40). Why five stones? If God was so powerful and David was so accurate, wouldn't one stone have been sufficient?

Allow me to give these five stones metaphorical meanings. Let them stand for prayer, protection, power, praise and perspective.

Prayer. David took his problem to the Lord. Indeed the source of all spiritual strength when doing battle with the giants in our lives is God. We are engaged in spiritual warfare, and we have spiritual weapons at our disposal whenever we do battle. "The weapons we fight with are not the

weapons of the world. On the contrary, they have divine power to demol-
ish strongholds" (2 Corinthians 10:4). The weapons in the Christian's arse-
nal are prayer and the Word of God. Paul reminded us, "Take . . . the
sword of the Spirit, which is the word of God. And pray in the Spirit on all
occasions with all kinds of prayers and requests" (Ephesians 6:17-18). So, as
odd as it may sound, prayer is a weapon.

While the weaponry of our armed forces is technical and complex,
prayer is not. We do not need more information about prayer so much as
we need inspiration to launch this powerful missile at the enemy. But let
me remind you that a weapon is useless if it is not aimed toward its target.
And likewise prayer is useless if it is not directed specifically toward God
about the giants in our lives. Powerful prayers are specific prayers.

Protection. David did not need the armor Saul offered, because he had
other armor protecting him. It was the invisible shield of faith—the presence of God—that David needed. David affirmed, "The LORD . . . will
deliver me from the hand of this Philistine" (1 Samuel 17:37). He never
faced an attacker alone. God was always with him. It was the knowledge of
this that gave David the courage to face his giant.

While it was a hurtling stone's centrifugal force that killed Goliath, it
was courage that enabled David to face the Philistine giant in the first
place. It is much easier to face our giants knowing that God is with us, protecting us and bringing all the forces of heaven to our defense.

Power. David's power came not in his skill as a marksman with a sling
but through the authority of God. David said, "You come against me with
sword and spear and javelin, but I come against you in the name of the
LORD Almighty" (1 Samuel 17:45).

Our strength rests not in our expertise, skill or knowledge but in the
resources of God. When we do battle with the overwhelming obstacles in
our lives, we fight in the name of God and for his honor. It's like a police
officer directing traffic in a busy intersection. His authority and power
come not because he is a man or because he has been to traffic control
school but because he is a police officer. His uniform and badge give him
the authority to direct the cars. Likewise, for us it is not because of who we
are but because of *whose* we are that we have the authority and the power

to face down our giants. We are children of the King and we have the authority of the King. We represent his throne. We bear his name. We fight in his strength.

Praise. David fought for another reason. He said, "Today I will give the carcasses of the Philistine army to the birds of the air and the beasts of the earth, and the whole world will know that there is a God in Israel" (1 Samuel 17:46). David was not fighting so people would say, "Look at David— he's a great giant killer." He was fighting so people would say, "Look at God—he's a great God."

Often repeated in the Old Testament is the phrase "that the world will know there is a God." When we prevail against our giants, the world knows that God is God. God's name is as much in question as is ours. When we defeat our giants, God gets the glory—as only he should.

Perspective. David had seen God, so Goliath did not look so big. The shepherd boy declared, "This day the LORD will hand you over to me" (1 Samuel 17:46). Others said, "He's too big to hit"; David said, "He's too big to miss." With one flick of the wrist, the stone flew. Down came Goliath. David had just scored the greatest upset in history.

It is amazing what can happen when we focus on God instead of the giants in our lives. When we take the time to engage God through worship, study and prayer, we will be amazed at how insignificant our problems become. We not only see the throne of God

> Gaze at God and glance at our giants.

but we see life *from* the throne of God. That perspective makes all the difference in the world.

How do we gain victory over our giants? Gaze at God and glance at our giants.

Acknowledge That the Battle Is the Lord's

Have you ever wondered how David mustered up the courage to face the nine-foot Goliath with just a slingshot? David answered the question forcefully when he confronted Goliath in combat. "The battle is the LORD's," he said (1 Samuel 17:47).

We can tackle any giant when we know for sure that the battle is the Lord's.

Could it be that many believers today are worn out because they are trying to fight God's battles in their own strength and with their own resources? Many of us need to resign as the general manager of the universe. We need to hear what God said to David: "I don't intend you to fight this battle. Just relax. If you're my child, I'll fight the battles."

God has never lost a battle. He always wins in the end. When we fight from God's side, it's like reading the last chapter of a novel and finding out that the good guy wins. Now we know it's going to end all right. We can relax through the story.

Jeris Bragan was imprisoned in the Tennessee State Prison. He knows firsthand that prison is a dreadful place to be, especially for young men who are small in stature. They're easily victimized by the bullies who roam every prison like wild animals in search of prey.

Bragan was surprised one day when he noticed two young brothers, both small in stature, fearlessly walking the prison yard. When he asked another prisoner why nobody ever bothered them, the prisoner laughed and asked, "Have you ever seen their father?"

Their father was a tough mountain man from east Tennessee who intentionally got himself arrested and sent to prison so he could look after his sons. He didn't baby them; he expected them to conduct themselves like men. But he also let it be known that anybody who attacked his sons would have to deal with him.

After three years, the father was paroled and left his sons behind. But they were safe. Nobody doubted the father would come back in a hurry if his sons needed him.

This remarkable, self-sacrificing father reminds me of God. We're all "prisoners," trapped in a world of powerful, threatening giants. But in the incarnation of Jesus Christ, God has joined us in our "prison" to help us fight and defeat these destructive giants.

How do we slay a giant? Whether our giant is the stronger team that we meet in the state finals of a basketball tournament or a Philistine named Goliath or sin issues in our life or a thousand other monsters, we can be victorious by taking the battle to the giant, fighting in God's power.

Study Questions

   1. Describe the giants you are now facing.

   2. In what ways do you need to take the battle to your giants?

   3. Our first job is to attack these items right in front of us, not what are merely distant thoughts. Name three action steps you need to take against your giants.

   4. David took five stones with him into battle. What "stones" do you need to take into battle against your giants?

   5. What does the statement "Gaze at God and glance at your giants" mean to you?

   6. What is God's role in fighting the giants in your life?

Nine

When You Face
an Impossibility

George Danzig was a senior at Stanford University during the Depression. All the seniors knew they'd be joining unemployment lines when the class graduated. There was a slim chance that the top person in the class might get a teaching job, but that was about it. George was not at the head of his class, but he hoped that if he were able to achieve a perfect score on the final exam, he might be given a job.

He studied so hard for the exam that he arrived late to class. When he got to class, the others were already hard at work. He was embarrassed and just picked up his paper and slunk to his desk. He sat down and worked the eight problems on the test paper, then he started on the two written on the board. Try as he might, he couldn't solve either of them. He was devastated. Out of ten problems, he had missed two for sure. But just as he was about to hand in the paper, he took a chance and asked the professor if he could have a couple of days to work on the two he had missed. He was surprised when the professor agreed.

George rushed home and plunged into those equations with a vengeance. He spent hours and hours, but he could find the solution for only one of them. He never could solve the other. It was impossible. When he turned in the test, he knew he had lost all chance of a job. That was the darkest moment of his life.

The next morning a pounding on the door awakened George. It was his mathematics professor, very excited. "George, George," he kept shouting, "you've made mathematics history!"

George didn't know what his professor was talking about. The professor explained. Before the exam, he had encouraged the class to keep trying in spite of setback and failure. "Don't be discouraged," he had counseled. "Remember, there are classic problems that no one can solve. Even Einstein was unable to unlock their secrets." He then wrote two of those problems on the blackboard. George had come to class late and missed those opening remarks. He didn't know the problems on the board were impossible to solve. He thought they were part of his exam and was determined that he could work them. And he solved one!

He did the impossible.

That very morning the professor made George Danzig his assistant. He taught at Stanford until his retirement.

Like George Danzig, Moses and the children of Israel were faced with an unsolvable problem—an impossibility. They had escaped the torture and abuse of Egyptian slavery, but now Pharaoh was leading his massive army in pursuit of the Israelites. When they arrived at the Red Sea, the Israelites were hemmed in. With mountains on each side, the Red Sea in front of them and the angry Egyptian army behind them, they were trapped. Their luck had run out.

Let's assess the situation. From their vantage point, they could see the Egyptians, reminding them of Egypt and their past. And interestingly enough, just like us, all they could remember about their past were the good things—"the good old days." They could not remember the shackles, the backbreaking labor or the taskmaster's whip.

Not only could they see back but also they could see forward—beyond the Red Sea. The land across the Red Sea represented their future: a future free of bondage and suffering, a future filled with hope and laughter.

The water, however, stretched out immediately before them. The Red

Sea represented their unsolvable problem. You could say the Red Sea reminded the Israelites of their human limitations. Like the Berlin Wall during the Cold War, it presented these people with no hope of escape.

It was their darkest moment.

How did they try to solve their unsolvable problem? Where did they turn for a solution?

What happened next was like a three-act play. In scene one the Israelites spoke to Moses; in scene two Moses spoke to the people; and in scene three God spoke to Moses. It was a defining moment for Moses and the children of Israel.

Fear Debilitates, While Faith Invigorates

"As Pharaoh approached, the Israelites looked up, and there were the Egyptians, marching after them. They were terrified and cried out to the LORD. They said to Moses, 'Was it because there were no graves in Egypt that you brought us to the desert to die? . . . It would have been better for us to serve the Egyptians than to die in the desert!' " (Exodus 14:10-12).

I heard the story of a 747 jetliner taxiing down the runway with the passengers all buckled up for takeoff. A voice came over the speakers in the cabin: "Good morning, ladies and gentlemen. This is your captain speaking. Welcome aboard Flight 22, headed for London's Heathrow Airport. We will climb to a cruising altitude of thirty thousand feet and will travel at an air speed of 660 miles per hour. Our flight plan will take us across Canada, Greenland, Iceland and over the tip of Ireland. Our flying time will be about nine hours. As soon as we are airborne the flight attendants will be serving you breakfast. We'll take off . . . just as soon as I can get up the nerve!"

I'm sure this event never happened, but its humor reminds us that to be human is to know fear. The children of Israel were terrified. They were being pressed in on all sides and they were scared out of their wits. Unsolvable problems and impossible situations have a tendency to do that, don't they?

When one is faced with impossibilities, fear is an unwelcome companion, cutting the life out of living. It has the ability to slap shackles on one's life, as it did to the Israelites, to keep the one who wears the chains bound up in frustration and hopelessness. And it does not restrict itself to the individual but, like a virus, can be transmitted to others.

Fear distorts perception of reality. It caused the children of Israel to believe that Egypt and its oppression would be better than Canaan and its hope. It prompts a man to imagine that the boss wanting

> Fear distorts perception of reality.

to see him in her office means that he is going to be fired. It persuades a wife to believe that when her husband is late coming home he is in the back of an ambulance. Most of our fears are unfounded, even when we are faced with seemingly impossible situations. We can agree with Mark Twain, who supposedly said, "I have known a great many troubles, but most of them never happened."

The children of Israel became whiners. Like the mariners who pleaded with Christopher Columbus to return to Europe before they reached the New World, the children of Israel wanted to turn around and go back to Egypt without discovering the new life of freedom and hope. Fear has a way of making cowards of us all.

Fear causes us to forget what God has done. The people of Israel had forgotten the plagues and the torture and the abuse. They had forgotten how God had miraculously delivered them from their bondage. They had forgotten how God had led them toward their homeland with the promise that they would experience a new life.

Fear blinds us to what God is seeking to accomplish. It sways us to trust in our human reasoning, which is often faulty when we are under the pressure of an impossibility.

Fear deafens us to God's voice. God is saying, "Fear not. Trust me." But we can't hear it for the distracting noise of timidity.

The Lord Will Win If We Surrender

There are many paradoxes in the Christian life: We die in order to live. We give in order to receive. We lose our life in order to find it. We are bound to Christ in order to be free in Christ. And in relation to the impossibilities in life, we have to surrender ourselves in order for the Lord to win.

Moses commanded the people, "Do not be afraid. Stand firm and you will see the deliverance the LORD will bring you today. The Egyptians you see today you will never see again. The LORD will fight for you; you need only to be still" (Exodus 14:13-14). It must have been very difficult to stand still when the enemy was breathing down their necks. Moses' instruction reads like a line in a war movie: "Don't shoot until you see the whites of their eyes." For the children of Israel, the instruction was to not flinch, to stand still, to wait.

It was a test of obedience. Human nature wants to look frantically for the nearest escape route when attacked. Many, when in a fix, want to bail out, to flee. Many times we act foolishly, engaging in inappropriate behavior, adhering to faulty advice, spending energy in futile efforts. When what we need to do is nothing. That's right. We simply need to stand still, to wait awhile.

Moses' order to be still was also a test of faith. We know the outcome. We have read the final chapter in this story. But remember that the Israelites had not heard from God that he would part the sea so they could walk on dry land to the other side. They were simply instructed to wait without knowing what would come next.

Often we hear the instruction "Don't just stand there; do something." The fact is, when confronted with difficulty and impossibility, God's instruction is often "Don't just do something; stand there."

Yes, stand there and surrender the impossibility to the Lord. Let him take it up in his power. Let him deal with it in his timing. Let him fight it in his strength. Let him handle it in his way.

> **"Don't just do something; stand there."**

Bruce Larsen counseled people for many years in his office in New York City. A large number of people struggled to surrender their lives to Christ. Often when someone was wrestling with this decision, he would suggest that they walk with him from his office down to the RCA building on Fifth Avenue. In the entrance of that building is a gigantic statue of Atlas, who, with all his muscles straining, is holding the world upon his shoulders. There he is, the most powerfully built man in the world, and he can barely stand up under this burden. "Now that's one way to live," Larsen would point out to his companion, "trying to carry the world on your shoulders. But now come across the street with me."

On the other side of Fifth Avenue stands Saint Patrick's Cathedral, and there behind the high altar is a little shrine of the boy Jesus, perhaps eight or nine years old, and with no effort he is holding the world in one hand. Larsen's point was illustrated graphically.

We have a choice. We can carry the world on our shoulders or we can give it up to the Lord. We can fight our battles on our own or let the Lord fight our battles for us. We can face our impossibilities and probably be defeated, or we can surrender them to the Lord and win.

The choice is ours.

Praying Is Ineffective When the Time Calls for Action

We can assume only two positions when we come into the presence of God. The first position is on our knees, saying, "God, be merciful to me, a sinner." The second is on our feet, saying, "Here am I! Send me."

What beautiful pictures of the Christian life—on our knees in confession and on our feet in response to God's call! One is a picture of prayer; the other is a picture of action. One is in obedience to the command "Attention!" The other is in obedience to the command "Forward, march!" The fact is, we need to assume both positions in turning impossibilities into possibilities, in transforming unsolvable problems into solvable problems. We need to pray, but we can't stay on our knees forever. God's ultimate call is to go forward.

The Sunday-school teacher asked one of the boys in his class, "Do you say a prayer before you eat at your house?" "No," the boy responded. "We don't have to. My mother is a good cook!" In his misguided understanding the young man nevertheless expressed an often-forgotten truth of the Bible: there are times when we do not need to pray. In fact there are times when we *should not* pray. This is what God said to Moses: "Why are you crying out to me? Tell the Israelites to move on. Raise your staff and stretch out your hand over the sea to divide the water so that the Israelites can go through the sea on dry ground" (Exodus 14:15-16). This moment defined Moses' life because, I believe, he thought God was going to rain down destruction on the Egyptians as the Israelites stood and watched. The Israelites would not have to lift a finger. God would do everything.

A delicate balance always exists between standing still and moving forward, between waiting and walking, between praying and acting. We have a lot of "sweet-and-low" Christians. They are *sweet* in praying but *low* in action. A danger to avoid is the tendency to allow prayer to become a substitute for work. Prayer is not the ultimate end of the Christian life. The ultimate end of our Christian lives is to bear fruit and glorify God. Prayer is simply a means to that end. Prayer is essential and prayer is good, but unless we rise from our knees to obediently follow the Lord, prayer is a farce.

So God ordered Moses and the children of Israel, "Move forward."

"Move forward?" the people replied timidly.

"That's right, move forward."

"But God, there is a big sea in our way. Don't you see it, God?"

True, a sea stood in their path. God saw it. But God didn't want the Israelites to see the sea; he wanted them to see *him*. He wanted his people to see what he could do. And the only way they could see his greatness and power was when they moved forward.

The events that unfolded at the Red Sea defined not only Moses; they also defined the Israelites. The Red Sea was an impossible barrier for them to cross. They would move forward in faith, the sea would part, and this story would be told from one generation to the next. It would become their rallying cry, like "Remember the Alamo" was for Texans in their fight against Mexico and "Remember Pearl Harbor" was for Americans in World War II. The Israelites would forever say, "Remember the Red Sea."

The story of the Red Sea can define us as well. It instructs us on what to do when faced with an impossibility. We all face "Red Sea" experiences. At those times we have the opportunity to allow fear to turn to faith and cowardice to courage. When we go on, we learn some of God's toughest principles.

God's power is given in direct proportion to our obedience. As we move forward obediently, God's power is given for us to fulfill our calling.

God's light is provided as we need it. It is like the light from a car's headlights. God doesn't shine the light down the length of the road; he shines it just far enough ahead for us to keep moving.

> God's power is given in direct proportion to our obedience.

God's miracles are provided as we expect them. When did the water part? The water parted when the Israelites put their feet into the sea. When their faith was displayed, the miracle occurred. It has always been that way. It will be that way in our lives as well.

God's Glory Is of Greater Importance Than Our Comfort and Convenience

This lesson is perhaps the most difficult of all to learn. One can't help but see it written at every turn in the Red Sea story:

> I will gain glory for myself through Pharaoh and all his army, and the Egyptians will know that I am the LORD. (Exodus 14:4)

> I will gain glory through Pharaoh and all his army, through his chariots and his horsemen. The Egyptians will know that I am the LORD when I gain glory through Pharaoh, his chariots and his horsemen. (verses 17-18)

> The Israelites went through the sea on dry ground, with a wall of water on their right and on their left. That day the LORD saved Israel from the hands of the Egyptians, and Israel saw the Egyptians lying dead on the shore. And when the Israelites saw the great power the LORD displayed against the Egyptians, the people feared the LORD and put their trust in him and in Moses his servant. (verses 29-31)

God's glory is intrinsic to his nature. God's glory is evident throughout the world. But there are times when God wishes to demonstrate his glory through feats or acts. This was one of those times. God's reputation was on the line. The reason the children of Israel were hemmed in was so God could be glorified.

Remember that. At times individuals, families and churches get hemmed in, confronted with an unsolvable problem. The reason is so God can be glorified. So that a watching world will know that God is God. And so that a fearful people can say, "What a God!"

The greatest problem about getting God's glory across to the world at such impossible moments is that it has to go through us. We like to quote the verse "My God will meet all your needs according to his glorious riches in Christ Jesus" (Philippians 4:19). But then an impossibility arises in our lives and we collapse. We panic. We turn and run. And everybody at work and at home knows it. Then people say, "Some kind of God you've got! You don't even trust him yourself." God is glorified when we believe in him, when we rest in his full assurance.

At those impossible moments our reputation is not all that's on the line; God's reputation is on the line too. As odd as it may seem, God's reputation depends on our faith and trust. Let's not let him down.

Study Questions

1. How do you attempt to solve your unsolvable problems?

2. Where do you turn for help when faced with difficulties?

3. What present events or situations are causing you to be fearful?

4. How has fear caused you to forget what God has done previously in your life?

5. How is obedience evidenced in your life?

6. How do you practice the command "Don't just do something; stand there"?

7. Presently, what situations are you just praying about when you should be acting?

8. Describe the times when God has performed a miracle in your life.

9. What role did your faith play when God acted?

10. How does God's reputation depend on your faith and trust?

Ten

When You Are Hurting

*B*etween flights at an airport, a traveler went to a lounge and bought a small package of cookies. Then she sat down and began reading a newspaper. Gradually she became aware of a rustling noise. From behind her paper, she was flabbergasted to see a neatly dressed man helping himself to her cookies. Not wanting to make a scene, she leaned over and took a cookie herself.

A minute or two passed and then came more rustling. He was helping himself to another cookie! By this time, they had come to the end of the package, but she was so angry that she didn't dare allow herself to say anything. Then, as if to add insult to injury, the man broke the remaining cookie in two, pushed half across to her and ate the other half.

Still fuming some time later when her flight was announced, the woman opened her handbag to get her ticket. To her shock and embarrassment, there she found her unopened package of cookies!

Stephen Grellet, a French missionary, is credited with saying, "I expect to pass through this world but once; and any good thing therefore that I can do, or any kindness that I can show to any fellow-creature, let me do it now; let me not defer or neglect it, for I shall not pass this way again."[1]

Whether it's sharing cookies or sharing an endearing remark, kindness is not an inconvenience to be avoided but a characteristic to be embraced.

Sometimes it is as simple as giving a pleasant smile or offering a warm handshake or sending a thank-you note or assisting a neighbor with a household project or being with a friend in distress or inviting someone to dinner or accepting a castaway. Ella Wheeler Wilcox wrote:

> So many gods, so many creeds,
> So many paths that wind and wind,
> While just the art of being kind
> Is all the sad world needs.[2]

A king expressed one of the most beautiful acts of kindness to a hurting outcast. For years Saul had hunted David like he was big game. Now Saul was dead and David had been crowned king of Israel. It was common practice in those days to exterminate all members of a previous dynasty to prevent any descendant from seeking the throne. Yet David's response was quite the contrary. He asked, "Is there anyone still left of the house of Saul to whom I can show kindness for Jonathan's sake?" (2 Samuel 9:1).

Kindness often smacks of softness. What David was expressing was a deeper demonstration of love. David had made a promise to Jonathan, his beloved friend and the son of Saul, that he would show kindness to the remaining members of Saul's household (see 1 Samuel 20:15-16). David now intended to keep that promise.

Finding the only remaining member of Saul's family was not a simple matter, but David located a grandson by the name of Mephibosheth, the son of Jonathan. He was crippled, living in poverty in a remote and barren corner of the kingdom. Brought to the palace, the young man hobbled into the throne room of the powerful king. I'm sure that when he appeared before David he expected the worse: *I'm going to be killed because Saul was my grandfather.*

But notice David's reaction: "Don't be afraid . . . for I will surely show you kindness for the sake of your father Jonathan. I will restore to you all the land that belonged to your grandfather Saul, and you will always eat at my table" (2 Samuel 9:7). David's action was not just a token gesture; it was extravagant—symbolic of his love for Jonathan. It was an act of grace—symbolic of God's love for David. His was a demonstration of love toward a man who had not earned it and would never be able to repay it. David, the strong and famous king, reached out to Mephibosheth, the cripple and outcast, and expressed kindness to him like he had never known before.

Mephibosheth must have felt tremendous relief at that moment. Expecting a sword to sever his head from his body, he heard unbelievable words of acceptance from the king. I wish I could have seen Mephibosheth's face at that moment—his defining moment.

With a Simple Word, Dignity Was Restored

The crippled Mephibosheth was an outcast, a vestige of the previous dynasty. Upon hearing David's words of grace, "Mephibosheth bowed down and said, 'What is your servant, that you should notice a dead dog like me?' " (2 Samuel 9:8). To Israelites, a dog was the most repulsive animal imaginable. On top of that, anything dead was considered vile and unclean. Mephibosheth thought of himself as a man of shame.

As he lay prostrate before the king in his moment of greatest vulnerability, perhaps the name-calling of a lifetime came flooding over him. Maybe he heard again the humiliating taunts of those who found him worthless and despicable. Probably he expected the disdain to which he had become accustomed.

Crippled. An outcast. Dead dog. Man of shame. David never spoke such words. Instead David said, "Where is this son?" (2 Samuel 9:4 NCV). One wonders how long it had been since Mephibosheth was called a son. Words have a way of changing us, don't they?

My dad traveled a lot, buying shoes for the shoe store he and my mother owned and operated. On some of his overnight trips he would take someone with him for company. Sometimes it was one of us children. Sometimes it was an African American man named Willie.

On one overnight trip Daddy pulled into a motel to stay the night. Daddy and Willie walked to the front desk and requested a room for the two of them. Looking at Daddy, the desk clerk said, "I can give you a room, but I will not give one to him," then pointed toward Willie.

"If he can't stay, then I won't stay," answered my father.

They walked out.

Out in the parking lot Willie said, "Mr. Ezell, you can stay in that room and I'll sleep here in the van. I'll be all right."

"No," replied Daddy. "If they won't let you stay in that motel, then I won't stay either. You are like family to me."

They both slept in the van that night.

At my dad's funeral Willie related this story to me. He said that my dad's words changed his life. For years he had thought of himself as second-class and second-rate. But when Daddy said, "You are like family to me," it raised his self-esteem.

I suspect that David's words changed Mephibosheth's life too. Words have a powerful way of bringing healing and restoration. Whoever said "Sticks and stones may break my bones, but words will never hurt me" lied. Unkind words can damage, while kind words can lead one to wholeness.

Someone Reached Out to Him

Mephibosheth's life had been one of rejection. When Saul and Jonathan were killed in battle, the nurse who cared for the infant Mephibosheth fled in fear, dropping the baby. Mephibosheth was left crippled for the rest of his life. He lived in obscurity and fear. He felt lost, forgotten and unimportant.

David, in one magnificent gesture of kindness, reached out to him and restored him to an exalted position. "You can eat at my table," David invited. Notice that four times in this short chapter we are told that Mephibosheth ate at David's table (2 Samuel 9:7, 10-11, 13). The castaway knew the wonderful feeling of acceptance. He knew the joy of being drawn into a family. He knew the warmth of love. He knew the contentment that comes when someone cares.

While traveling in Switzerland, I was sitting at a crowded bus stop. Out of the corner of my eye I noticed a little boy about six or seven years old ambling toward the bus stop. He appeared to be walking aimlessly without a care in the world. When he looked behind him, though, he realized that he was walking alone. Fear came over him and he began to cry out, "Somebody! Somebody!" As he got closer, I could see that he was a Down syndrome child. The louder he called for "Somebody!" the wider the people parted to avoid this child. He began to look around at the people almost as if he were a cornered animal. "Somebody! Somebody!" he shouted as his face grew whiter with fright.

I said to myself, *Somebody ought to do something.* About that time the bus pulled up and people started to get on while this boy kept yelling, "Somebody!" Then out of the crowd came a young woman who answered, "Somebody." She gathered the boy up in her arms, held him tightly and quieted him by whispering, "Somebody. Somebody."

By now I had boarded the bus. As I waited for the bus to pull away from the curb, I saw another woman running toward the woman holding the Down syndrome child. At that moment I realized the second woman was the mother of the child, while the first woman was just a kind person who saw someone hurting and reached out in love.

Isn't it funny how we tend to stay away from the Mephibosheths of the world—the hurting, the handicapped and the marginalized? Yet they need to be held in the same esteem as anyone else. They, like all people, matter to God.

David restored Mephibosheth from a place in the wilderness to a place at his table. From a place of barrenness to a place of honor. From a place with no pastureland to a place of plenty. From a place of hurt to a place of happiness, he brought him into the very palace of the king. For years Mephibosheth had been crying out, "Somebody! Somebody!" The somebody who reached out to him was none other than the king. David not only helped him but took him in his arms, adopting him as a son.

Think about life in the kingdom of God for a moment. Why does the king of heaven adopt us into his family? Is it because of our personal goodness? Our likable personality? Our compelling charm? Our stupendous talents? If you're tempted to answer yes, think again. My place and your place at the King of kings's table serves as a reminder of how God takes people whom others would have abandoned and reaches out to us and grants us a place in his presence.

Kindness Provides for People's Needs

David was not through with Mephibosheth. He had given him a new identity and a new position. Now he was going to provide for his needs—food, shelter and financial resources. David said, "I will restore to you all the land that belonged to your grandfather Saul" (2 Samuel 9:7). Mephibosheth inherited the wealth of a king. It was like winning the lottery and having a rich uncle leave you his fortune all in a single day. It was too good to be true.

Kindness is more than giving a pat on the back and saying, "Have a good day." Kindness is visible and active. It moves beyond the spiritual and the emotional to the physical and practical. It concentrates on filling needs and healing hurts.

David could have ignored Mephibosheth. Who would have blamed him? Who would have confronted him if he had? But David did not ignore the outcast.

> Kindness is visible and active. It moves beyond the spiritual and the emotional to the physical and practical.

What about the people like Mephibosheth all around us? Some with broken hearts, others with damaged emotions, many with crushed spirits, quite a few with shattered souls, and a lot with physical needs. Are we ignoring them like a ding in our car door? Like garbage in the Dumpster?

My wife and I moved into our previous home on Independence Day weekend. We were busy unpacking boxes and unloading furniture when I heard a knock on the front door. When I opened the door, I faced a wiry man wearing blue jean cutoffs and no shirt and holding a Budweiser. I thought he was a transient looking for a handout. He introduced himself, "Hi, I'm Ralph, your neighbor across the street. We're having a pool party. Won't you take a break and come over?"

"Thanks, but no thanks," I said. "We've got a lot of boxes to unpack." Somehow I couldn't envision the Baptist preacher in his first week on the job going to a party with strangers where beer was being served.

The next week I was in my driveway trying to get my lawn mower started. I'm not very mechanical and the few tools I had weren't getting the job done.

Ralph drove by and waved. In a few minutes he came over with a big, red toolbox. It was one of those Craftsman toolboxes and it contained every tool one could imagine. "Thought you might need a hand," he said.

"Well, yes. I sure do."

In a matter of minutes the mower was running.

"You must build a lot of things with those tools," I said as Ralph was putting his last tool away in the red toolbox.

"Naw," he replied, "mostly good neighbors."

The watchword of today's society is "Don't get involved." But at the heart of a kind person is involvement. Like Ralph did for me, David met Mephibosheth's need. He was willing to risk helping him even if others didn't understand.

It is time we moved from pious platitudes to practical involvement. From merely standing for what is right to doing what is right. From just carrying a placard to city hall to carrying a casserole next door. From our religious activities to genuine Christian service.

When he was in his seventies, the late Charles M. Schwab was the victim of a nuisance suit. The sum for which he was sued was extremely large. Schwab, who could have settled for a fraction of the amount named, refused to do so. He let the case run its legal course. He won it easily. Before leaving the stand, he asked the court's permission to say a few words.

> It is time we moved from pious platitudes to practical involvement.

"I'd like to say, here, in a court of law, and speaking as an old man, that nine-tenths of my troubles are traceable to my being kind to others. Look, you young people; if you want to steer away from trouble, be hard-boiled. Be quick with a good loud *no* to anyone and everyone. If you follow this rule, you'll be seldom molested as you tread life's pathway. Except," and the great man paused, a grand smile lighting his kindly features, "Except—you'll have no friends, you'll be lonely—and you won't have any fun!"[3]

William Wordsworth was right when he wrote:

On that best portion of a good man's life,
His little, nameless, unremembered, acts
Of kindness and of love.[4]

Kindness Originates from the Heart of God

In every walk of life it is important to follow that old Texas maxim "Hug your friends tight but your enemies tighter—hug 'em so tight they can't wiggle." That's what God does for us. God is kind because he cannot be otherwise. It is essential to his nature. And kindness becomes a part of our conduct because our character as Christians is rooted in God. The poet Robert Burns stated:

> The heart benevolent and kind
> The most resembles God.[5]

Let's not overlook the verse where David asked, "Is there no one still left of the house of Saul to whom I can show *God's* kindness?" (2 Samuel 9:3, emphasis added). David's life had been spared on numerous occasions. He had fought the giant Goliath and won. He had escaped the dangers of wild beasts. His life had been redeemed from the pit of pain and hunger and desertion more than a few times. All because of the kindness of God. Now David wanted to share that kindness with others. Those who have been touched by the grace of God want to pass it on.

What David did for Mephibosheth, God does for us. Just as the king brought the outcast into the palace and made him a son, so God adopts us into his family. You and I are Mephibosheths. The similarities between his life and ours are astounding. Before we came into a relationship with the Father, we spent our lives distancing ourselves from him because of our brokenness and shame. We feared that entering his presence would bring judgment upon our heads. When finally we lay trembling at his feet, he touched us and said, "Don't be afraid." He lifted us up and said, "I'm going to give back to you everything you ever lost because of sin. I'm going to give you an inheritance, blessings and riches in the heavenly places. But more than that, I want you forever in my presence eating at my table, and I'm going to call you my child." And when we protested, "But why would you care about a cripple like me?" he answered, "Because I know your brother Jesus. For his sake I'm doing all this for you."

Study Questions
1. What is the kindest act anyone has ever done for you?
2. In what ways do you feel marginalized?
3. Describe a time when someone's words affirmed you.

4. How would you define *grace?*

5. How has grace been demonstrated to you?

6. How have you demonstrated grace to others?

7. How can you get involved with those less fortunate than you?

8. How can you show kindness to those around you?

9. Describe the similarities between David's graciousness toward Mephibosheth and God's graciousness toward you.

10. When we know God's grace, we want to pass it on. What practical ways can we share God's grace?

Eleven

When Your Health Fails

*R*ecently my church was in the midst of a building expansion project and a major capital stewardship campaign. In addition to my regular duties, directing these ventures turned a busy schedule into an unbearable one. There were not enough hours in the day to pull it all together.

One Monday morning I arrived at the church in time to film a videotape for use in the capital campaign. I took my place and began reading the TelePrompTer for the first scene. Wilbur, one of my best friends, was assisting with the videotaping crew. He said, "Rick, as I have watched you read your lines, I have noticed that your left eye is not blinking. The right eye blinks, but your left eye is always open." When he commented on my eye, I recalled that the day before this eye had hurt, but I hadn't thought much about it then. Even when Wilbur mentioned it now, I passed it off as something that would go away.

But it didn't.

It required all day to film the video. And with each setup, as I read from the TelePrompTer at different locations throughout the church, Wilbur would remind me, "Rick, your eye is not blinking."

As the day went on, Wilbur became more and more worried. "You had better get it checked out. You need to see a doctor."

"Oh, Wilbur," I said each time, "I'll be all right."

As the day dragged on, my eye began hurting, then hurting some more. And to make matters worse, I was losing control of the left side of my face. The left side of my mouth was now numb. I finally became alarmed.

By the end of the day, I decided that I had better schedule an appointment with my doctor.

The next day, after the examination, my doctor's diagnosis was that I had Bell's palsy, a condition in which the nerve going through the skull to the side of one's face becomes inflamed or blocked. He indicated that the mild paralysis and numbness would clear up in four to eight weeks. And he was right.

Since prior to this time I had not been sick except for an occasional cold or flu, this experience helped me to understand the sense of concern and helplessness that overtakes people when their body does not respond as it is supposed to. I walked away with a greater appreciation and sensitivity toward those who are sick.

I began to see other things differently too. God reminded me that he was trying to get through to me. I had become so busy doing the work of God that I was not hearing the voice of God. I was reminded of my inadequacy without God.

Something similar happened to Naaman.

Naaman was like the chairman of the Joint Chiefs of Staff in his day. The Bible says, "Now Naaman was commander of the army of the king of Aram. He was a great man in the sight of his master and highly regarded, because through him the LORD had given victory to Aram. He was a valiant soldier" (2 Kings 5:1). Did you hear those descriptive words? Don't we desire people to utter these words about us? *Commander. Great. Highly regarded. Victorious. Valiant.* Here was a man who had power, position and prestige.

But—a three-letter conjunction. That small word changes everything.

Notice how verse 1 concludes: "But he had leprosy." Naaman could think about all of his accomplishments; he could enjoy his power and position and prestige; he could admire his home and his wealth; but these all seemed to vanish as he stared into the mirror each day. Each time he looked at himself there was something looking back that defined his life. He was a leper.

Consider Christopher Reeve. Movie star. Wealthy. Handsome. Winner of awards and honors. Adored by fans. *But.* Once he was known as Superman, with the power to bend steel bars, leap tall buildings and fly into the heavens, but now his life is defined by an aluminum wheelchair. Earthbound after falling off a horse, he is a paraplegic, and presently nothing can change that fact.

Nothing could change the fact that Naaman was a leper. Leprosy was the AIDS of Naaman's day, the most feared disease around. It was extremely contagious and, in many cases, incurable. In its worst forms leprosy led to death.

Lepers were isolated and humiliated. They were forced to wear torn clothing and shout, "Unclean, unclean!" anytime they encountered an uninfected person. Granted, Naaman's leprosy was probably in an early stage or simply a mild form. He had concealed it for a while, but now his clothing would not cover it. While people treated him respectfully, now nobody would touch him. The lack of touch hurt Naaman deeply.

When We Need a Touch

Like Naaman, we too long for a meaningful touch. Why is it that we squeeze the widow's hand at her husband's funeral? Why is it that we sympathetically pat the shoulder of the defeated athlete? Why do we bearhug a long-lost friend? Why is it that we hold our

> Touch conveys acceptance. Touch promotes health.

babies? Why is that when my daughter is sad, she says, "Hold me, Daddy"? Touch brings comfort. Touch conveys acceptance. Touch promotes health. Touch imparts wholeness.

I can't imagine going through life without being touched. I relish my wife holding my hand when we're walking down a dark street. I love back rubs. I appreciate someone patting me on the shoulder for a job well done. I long for the embrace of my daughter when I return from a trip away from home.

By the way, what is your leprosy? What is your illness? What problem are you trying to conceal? What hurt are you trying to cover up? What prevents you from getting close to other people? Where do you need to be touched?

I, too, like Naaman, have my disfigurements. For a while mine was Bell's palsy. At other times it is insecurity, bitterness, jealousy or perfectionist tendencies. I, too, have become proficient at covering up my problems. I need God's healing touch. While in my position as a pastor I pray for a lot of people, there are times when I need someone to pray for me. I hurt too.

So what do we do? Where do we find help? Where do we go for healing?

In a word, we go down. In our world we are encouraged to go up—and rewarded when we do so. But down is the way we must go if we are to find healing. Downward is the route we must take if we are going to feel the touch of God.

Notice the contrasts in Naaman's journey. Naaman, the commander-in-chief, found direction through a captive servant—his wife's slave. Naaman, the conqueror, found help in a conquered nation—Israel. Naaman, the highly regarded man, learned of his treatment from a lowly prophet—Elisha. Naaman, the wealthy and valiant soldier, was cured in a dirty river—the Jordan.

What can we learn from his downward descent?

We Need People Who Look Past Our Haughtiness to Our Hurt

"Now bands from Aram had gone out and had taken captive a young girl from Israel, and she served Naaman's wife. She said to her mistress, 'If only my master would see the prophet who is in Samaria! He would cure him of his leprosy' " (2 Kings 5:2-3). The servant of Naaman's wife had been taken hostage in an Aramean raid into Israel. Now she served in Naaman's home, tending to his wife's every need. She was not intimidated by Naaman's power, position or prestige. She saw his pain and told him where he could find help.

We need humble people in our lives who look past our outward appearance—past our job titles and bank accounts and houses—and see our loneliness and our hurt. We need people who will touch us at our point of need. We need people who will see our blind spots. We even need people who love us enough not to let us make stupid mistakes.

One time I had about had it with a person at church who was attacking me unmercifully and untruthfully. This tension was creating stress at home and frustration in every area of my life. I was mad. So I had lunch with my close friend Wilbur and splattered my anger all over him. Being the genuine, mature friend that he was, he let me erupt. I told him I was considering verbally attacking my offender from the pulpit. Tactfully, Wilbur pointed out to me how destructive such an attack would be. He loved me enough to prevent me from making a stupid mistake.

We need people in our lives (like Wilbur is for me) who will demonstrate the four Cs of loving relationships:

□ Concern—They speak the truth to us in love.

□ Commitment—They walk through the pain with us.

□ Confidentiality—They keep the struggles between us.

□ Consistency—They maintain regular contact with us.

In exhibiting these qualities trusted friends are saying, "I'm going to help you become the best you can be."

Everybody has balcony people and basement people in their lives. Balcony people encourage us; basement people exhaust us. Who are your balcony people? Who sustains and inspires you? Who looks beyond your outward appearance and sees your inward hurt? We all need someone who will touch us at our point of need and inspire us to be the best we can be.

We Need Places That Provide Us with Safety

"Naaman went to his master and told him what the girl from Israel had said. 'By all means, go,' the king of Aram replied" (2 Kings 5:4-5). Israel was a conquered nation. What did it have to offer? Militarily it did not present much of a threat, but spiritually it provided refuge.

In my community a program is in place for children who are lost or feel threatened. A poster with a white hand on red background was designed for them, and certain homes display the poster in their front windows. The sign indicates to lost and confused children that these homes are places of safety. If in danger, children know that they can get to a home with the hand in the window and find a caring adult who will protect them.

The church is a safe place. A place that gives caring embraces to those who come in contact with its ministries. A place that provides sanctuary from danger. Each week people come to our churches for a touch, fully knowing that they may not get touched again until they come back to church the next Sunday.

Israel was a safe place for Naaman. That's simple enough to understand. But before I leave this thought, I would like to point out that, though Naaman was in the right place, he was speaking to the wrong person. He first went to the king of Israel, but the king could not help him. In fact the king misunderstood his coming and thought Naaman was trying to pick a fight!

Many people come to the right place each Sunday—the church—but speak to the wrong person. They come to impress their friends with their exploits or to astound their classmates with their attire or to amaze the pastor with their credentials, and all the while they miss the main event. They talk to their friends, to their classmates, even to the pastor, but they don't talk to God. In fact it is becoming increasingly easy in Western Christianity to come to church and not pray a prayer to God or sing a song to God or hear a word from God. We can get caught up in the performance of a worship service and miss the encounter with God.

We need to talk with God when we attend church. He is the one who wants to heal us, to scoop us up in his arms and hug us.

We Need Prophets Who Will Point Us to the Cure
"When Elisha the man of God heard that the king of Israel had torn his robes, he sent him this message: 'Why have you torn your robes? Have the man come to me and he will know that there is a prophet in Israel' " (2 Kings 5:8). So Naaman went to Elisha in Samaria. Remember Samaria? If Israel was a second-rate country, Samaria was the armpit of the second-rate country. It was despised even by the Israelites.

When Naaman arrived at Elisha's dusty enclave, Elisha sent out his servant. To this point Naaman had been remarkably flexible and amiable, willingly traveling to the prophet's remote outpost to ask for the healing touch. But when Elisha's servant showed up at the door with the instructions for the cure, he was incensed.

Naaman was a big shot in his country and he wanted a welcoming committee to meet him at the door. I'm sure he thought the Israelites would roll out the red carpet with an impressive banquet honoring him, not to mention an esteemed doctor to heal him. But God does not always send blessings through the people we want. Often God chooses a lowly person to accomplish his healing.

If we look for God only in the spectacular, we may miss him in the mundane. God may use an ordinary, plain-vanilla approach to touch us and heal us. We may miss his blessing if we are looking for the extraordinary. Many have received the touch of God and the healing of his power, but because it was not spectacular, they have attributed it to coincidence or logic.

> God does not always send blessings through the people we want.

Naaman almost rejected his opportunity for healing by becoming angry because Elisha did not show up to greet him at the door. Elisha hadn't read the book on protocol when meeting foreign dignitaries. But while he may not have had tact, he had a treatment.

We Need a Prescription That Will Lead to a Healing

Elisha's prescription for healing was bizarre. "Go, wash yourself seven times in the Jordan, and your flesh will be restored and you will be cleansed" (2 Kings 5:10).

That's crazy, thought Naaman. *Seven baths in a dirty river? Why, we have rivers in Aram that are better than the Jordan.* Naaman doubted that God's prescription for healing would really do anything. Naaman did not realize that the power was not in the water but in his obedience to God's command.

Naaman continued to doubt when he entered the Jordan and came up still a leper. God reminded him that when he says seven, six will not do.

What about us? When God asks for seven times, do we try to get by with only five or six? God wants us to go the distance; will we? God is not trying to tie conditions to his healing, but rather he is testing our obedience. We must believe that God's way is better than our own. We may not always understand his way of working, but by humbly obeying, we will receive his blessings.

Let me retrace Commander-in-Chief Naaman's downward descent. First, he received instructions from a slave girl to go to a second-rate, conquered country. In that second-rate country he was to go to a lowly prophet who lived in the armpit of the country. This lowly prophet did not bother to greet him at the door but instead sent a servant. The servant gave him instructions to go to the dirty Jordan River and to bathe not once or twice but seven times.

To refresh your geographical understanding, let me remind you that the Jordan River (whose name means "the descender") flows through a rift valley. Its headwaters lie more than a thousand feet above sea level at the foot of Mount Hermon, while its mouth lies nearly thirteen hundred feet below sea level at the Dead Sea. So to go to the Jordan River was to go down—way down.

Why did Naaman have to descend in order to receive healing? For that matter, why must you and I? Why must we have a compliant attitude toward God's instructions? The apostle Peter answered that question:

> Clothe yourselves with humility toward one another, because,
>   "God opposes the proud
>   but gives grace to the humble."
> Humble yourselves, therefore, under God's mighty hand, that he may lift you up in due time. (1 Peter 5:5-6)

> **Sometimes we have to scrape bottom before we can start going up.**

Sometimes we have to scrape bottom before we can start going up. We have to look at death before we can see life. We have to taste pain before we can experience joy. God chooses to touch us most when we bow humbly before him.

Naaman was that low. He finally humbled himself in complete obedience to the instructions of God's messenger. And in doing so he was touched by God and healed in a way that did not fit his expectations. "He went down and dipped himself in the Jordan seven times, as the man of God had told him, and his flesh was restored and became clean like that of a young boy" (2 Kings 5:14).

Having experienced the grace of God, Naaman was changed not only physically but also spiritually. Naaman stood before Elisha and said, "Now I know that there is no God in all the world except in Israel. Please accept now a gift from your servant" (2 Kings 5:15). Naaman went from a sick man to a healed man, from an ungodly man to a godly man, from a lost man to a saved man, from a great man to a gracious man, and from a commander of men to a servant of God. Here was a man who had felt the touch of God and was changed. Now and forever. It was his defining moment.

I need that healing. If we are honest with ourselves, we all desperately need the touch of God. We need to be open to God's unique ways of dealing with us.

Allow me to close this chapter by telling you about my friend Daryl. At thirty-five Daryl returned home to live with his parents. I had seen him at church for several Sundays holding on tightly to one of his parent's arms. I learned that his eyesight was fading. I wanted to get to know him, so I invited him to lunch. Over pizza and Cokes, he told me his story. He had been taken to church as a boy, but when he was grown up he had tried it all—drugs, alcohol, jobs, women. His pursuit of happiness led him further and further away from God. While living in Seattle, Washington, he had discovered that he was going blind. Most people would have lashed out at God, but here was a rare individual who through his experience saw God.

I invited Daryl to share his story at church. Those in attendance listened in awe and wonder. I'll never forget how Daryl closed his talk. He said, "I had to go blind before I could see God. I pray that what has happened to me will never happen to you. Unless . . ."—he paused for a moment to make sure everyone heard his final words—"unless that is what it takes for you to see God."

In a crisis, while our physical eyes are closed, our spiritual eyes are opened. It happened for Naaman. It happened for Daryl. It happened for me.

Issues with my eyes have been a constant in my life. In the fourth grade I discovered that I had to wear glasses. I did not want to wear glasses. Only sissies wore glasses, I thought. How could I play ball with glasses? When my mother and I picked up the glasses from the doctor, my mother asked the doctor what she should do since I was so adamant about not wearing the glasses. The doctor replied, "When you get home, show Rick where you are placing the glasses for safekeeping. You don't have to say anything about him wearing them. He knows he can see better with them. One day he will pick them up and start wearing them."

And you know what? I did.

It's a wonderful gift to see clearly and plainly. What's true physically is also true spiritually. As a result of Bell's palsy, I began to see God in a new light. I became refocused upon him and his working in my life. While it wasn't a pleasant lens to look through (what crisis is?), it provided a new vision of my need for God.

The turning point for me came as a choice. In the fourth grade it was the choice of wearing glasses or not. With my Bell's palsy it was the choice of seeing God or not. For Naaman it was the choice of being obedient or not. It seems like it's always a choice, doesn't it? For our spiritual and physical healing, it is the choice of humbling ourselves before God even in the midst of our crisis so he can touch us. It is the choice of being obedient to his instructions even if it means washing ourselves in a dirty river just because God says so. When we choose God, we see God.

Study Questions

1. List your most admirable qualities.

2. With what you know of leprosy, how do you think people with this disease feel? Put yourself in their place for a moment.

3. How do you like people to express affirmation toward you? Words? Service? Touch? Gifts?

4. In your present condition, where do you hurt the most?

5. Name three people who bring out the best in you.

6. What was your response when someone spoke prophetic words to you?

7. Naaman was told to dip seven times in the Jordan River in order to be healed. What would have been your reaction to such a demand?

8. It has been said that desperate times call for desperate measures. If you are desperate, what measures do you need to take for healing?

Twelve

When You Don't Get What You Want

As a preschooler, I was a Roy Rogers enthusiast. I wore a Roy Rogers cowboy hat, a Roy Rogers holster and a Roy Rogers belt. I even had Roy Rogers saddlebags for my bicycle. (I didn't have a horse, but I had an active imagination.) I was so caught up with Roy Rogers that I was upset with my parents because our last name did not start with an R. Since I had a first name that started with an R, if I'd had a last name that started with an R, then the double Rs on my Roy Rogers paraphernalia could have stood for my name too. In fact I had all the Roy Rogers stuff I wanted except for one item. To be a full-fledged cowboy, I needed Roy Rogers chaps.

When Christmas came around, I sent my letter off to Santa. It was different from my previous letters. They all contained a litany of gifts that I wanted. But not this year. "Dear Santa," I wrote, "all I want this Christmas is a pair of Roy Rogers chaps. Love, Ricky."

When I visited with Santa at the Sears store, he asked, "What do you want for Christmas?" I replied, "As my letter indicated, all I want for Christmas is a pair of Roy Rogers chaps." He assured me that the chaps were in the bag.

When Christmas came, I was confident that the chaps were under the tree. But when I tore off the paper to open my present and stuck my hand in the box, I knew something was wrong. The present wasn't soft like chaps; it was hard and cold. I pulled out the present and, to my chagrin, discovered not Roy Rogers chaps but an electric guitar. I began to cry, "Where are my Roy Rogers chaps?"

There are times when the one thing you want is the one thing you never get. Brad dreamed of pitching in the major leagues and performed well on his college team. But the scout said that while his breaking pitches were major-league stuff, his fastball just didn't have enough zip. Sarah wanted to move up the ranks in her firm, but while she possessed knowledge of the business, she lacked managerial skills. The promotion never came. Ted and Alice desperately wanted a child and were suited to be great parents. They prayed and waited, but no conception. I had gone through all the proper channels for getting Roy Rogers chaps. I never got Roy Rogers chaps. And I never learned to play the electric guitar.

The Christian life entails hoping and hurting, trying and failing, wanting but not always receiving. There are no guarantees for the fulfillment of our prayers, our dreams or our goals. Sometimes God says no.

And when he does, how do we respond? What if our request is denied or the door is slammed in our face or the dream dies? How do we react? What if God says, "I've given you my grace, and that is enough"? Will we be satisfied?

From heaven's perspective, grace *is* enough. If God did nothing more for us than to save us from hell, could we complain? If God saved our souls and left us to spend our lives in a distant Third World country, would he be unjust? If God grants us the riches of his heavenly kingdom, can we complain about earthly poverty?

But God has not left us with "just salvation." If we own a car, we are richer than 95 percent of the world's population. If we have eyes to see, hands to hold and legs to walk, then we ought to have the brains to know that we have received more than our share of blessings.

But there are those times when God, having heard our appeals, says,

"My grace is sufficient for you." We don't get the answer we want. Tell me, is God still a good God when he says no?

A Strange Gift

The apostle Paul wrestled with that question. He knew what no from God sounded like. He testified, "There was given me a thorn in my flesh" (2 Corinthians 12:7). But not the removal of the thorn.

> Tell me, is God still a good God when he says no?

A thorn in the flesh? This sort of affliction is more than a thorn you might get while picking roses; it is a stake on which a man is tortured. This thorn is more than the usual annoyances of life—more than a hangnail on the finger, more than a bad day with the kids, more than an unrelenting boss. A thorn is a tragedy, a broken dream, a sickness, an unshakable fear, a disability that dogs you for life. Theologically, "thorn" refers to some circumstance for which we didn't ask, which we pray to have removed and by which we are given the grace to keep going and behave in such a way that the Father will be glorified.

Granted, not everyone may experience a thorn in the flesh. Some may be so fortunate as to live without knowing the kind of pain and struggle that others face every day of their lives. I wish my Aunt Evelyn had been so lucky. For years she taught first grade, until crippling arthritis kept her from the classroom. But while this disease took the mobility in her hands, it did not take the joy from her heart. All the years I knew my aunt I never heard her complain even though many times I saw her grimace from the pain. A joy filled her heart that enabled her to live above the discomfort and frustration. She and Uncle Ottis took many trips and spent a lot of money trying to find a cure or at least relieve her pain, but to no avail. She lived the balance of her life with the thorn of arthritis. She never found a cure or relief.

While I know what troubled my aunt, I don't know what Paul's thorn in the flesh was. No one knows. But every time he had private thoughts, every time he entered a new town, every time he stepped in front of a mirror, every time he walked or tried to write, every time he stood to speak, he shuddered in pain. The thorn was omnipresent.

When All We Can Do Is Pray

The thorn pierced Paul's heart and became a matter of intense prayer. He said, "Three times I pleaded with the Lord to take it away from me" (2 Corinthians 12:8). This was no casual request. This was all-out earnest begging for God's intervention and removal of this stake in his heart. The intensity of his pain was matched by the intensity of his prayer.

He prayed three times, which is an echo of our Lord's prayer in the garden for the cup to be removed. For Jesus the cup was not removed, and he endured the nails of a cross. For Paul the thorn was not removed, and he endured the affliction of a stake.

God said no.

For Paul this denied request became his defining moment. If God had removed the thorn, Paul may never have embraced God's grace. No person ever articulated grace like Paul because no person ever appreciated grace like Paul.

The Fact of Sustaining Grace

Paul did not get the answer he wanted but the one God knew was best. Paul wrote, "He said to me, 'My grace is sufficient for you, for my power is made perfect in weakness' " (2 Corinthians 12:9). Interestingly, these are the only words of the risen Christ found in Paul's letters. Through them God gave Paul a wonderful promise: "I'm all you need." Paul wrote "He said" in the perfect tense, meaning that God said his grace was sufficient and ongoing.

God's gift to Paul was not the thorn; it was his grace. Sustaining grace is God's gift of courage and faith, his presence and strength, to face the tragedy, broken dream, sickness, unshakable fear or disability that dogs you.

I've often wondered why Aunt Evelyn was afflicted with such pain. She was so kind, so tender, so gracious. She made people feel special. I know why many of her former students returned to see he: she had left an indelible mark on their lives. She would have impacted so many more if she could have continued to teach, I've thought. But while healing grace never came to her, sustaining grace did. In spite of her crippled hands and wrecked body, her vibrant faith and enthralling love for life had a powerful impact on everyone she met. Like the apostle Paul, Aunt Evelyn discovered that God's grace is indeed sufficient.

Why doesn't God remove our thorns? Perhaps he wants us to lean on his grace and not on our strength. Why doesn't God remove the enemies from our life? Perhaps he wants us to love like he loves. Why doesn't God erase our physical flaws? Perhaps he wants us to know that we are loved in spite of our defects. Why doesn't God heal us? Perhaps he wants us to be sensitive to those who are weak and frail and ill. Why doesn't God make us a dynamic speaker or gifted singer or best-selling author? Perhaps he wants to remind us that the power is in the message, not the messenger.

We are filled with questions when it comes to suffering and pain and injustice. And when we associate God with the pain, the lack of answers becomes increasingly difficult to handle. In fact for many it leads to anger and bitterness. Why would God allow anyone to endure a life with a painful circumstance? Paul answered the question for us: "To keep me from becoming conceited" (2 Corinthians 12:7). Of all the things that God hates (and there are plenty of those), pride heads the list. A pride-filled demeanor communicates one's sense of self-sufficiency and corresponding lack of dependence on God. Max Lucado writes, "For all we don't know about thorns, we can be sure of this. God would prefer we have an occasional limp than a perpetual strut. And if it takes a thorn for him to make his point, he loves us enough not to pluck it out."[1]

Principles to Live By

Okay, God has every right to say no to us. And we know that his grace is sufficient for us. But how does that play out in everyday life? Good question. Here are some practical lessons about God's sustaining grace.

God's sustaining grace comes to us as we need it. In other words, we don't get to store up God's grace. We don't stash it away in a grace account. Scripture says, "Your strength will equal your days" (Deuteronomy 33:25).

Ron Hutchcraft tells of when his wife, Karen, was left bedridden for six months with hepatitis and he was left with the unsought title of Mr. Mom. With the needs of the house and the family suddenly piled on top of a relentless load of speaking, managing, broadcasting, counseling and fundraising, he was overwhelmed. "Lord," he prayed desperately, "I can't! I give up!"

"Good," God said, and every night for six months God sent dinner to their door as well as strength and help that Ron never could have imagined. Their pastor's wife knew how Ron depended on Karen. One day she asked, "How have you managed for five weeks without Karen?"

Ron responded, "I haven't managed for five weeks. I've managed for thirty-five days."

The sustaining grace of God was making the difference each day.

God's sustaining grace is often mediated through human instruments. God likes to employ the human instruments of family, friends, ministers and other caring persons to offer encouragement and assistance. Medications, therapy and counseling can also be God's agents of sustaining grace.

The using of others in the healing process is consistent with God's involvement with creation. God has delegated responsibility to human beings from the beginning. Many times when God wants something done, he will work through other people.

> Many times when God wants something done, he will work through other people.

God's sustaining grace is tailored for our individual needs. God's love in our lives is not one-size-fits-all. Our Father invites us to "approach the throne of grace with confidence, so that we may receive mercy and find grace to help us in our time of need" (Hebrews 4:16). God customizes his response to our specific pain, giving us the kind of healing balm we need.

God's sustaining grace in weakness enables us to become instruments of power in God's hands. I recall the many times I have finished speaking and wanted to cry. My delivery was terrible. My voice cracked. My grammar would have made my high-school English teacher shriek in pain. But miraculously God used me. People would say to me afterward, "You'll never know how that sermon touched my life." Was it my weakness with which they identified? Was it my humanness that became an encouragement to them? Or was it God using a broken and wounded vessel to demonstrate his power?

God's sustaining grace enables us to rise above our circumstances. God does not give us his grace simply so that we might *endure* our sufferings. Even unbelievers can manifest great endurance. God's grace equips us to rise above our tragedies, broken dreams, sickness, unshakable fears and disability and cause our afflictions to work for us in accomplishing good. God wants to build our character so that we are more like his Son. God's grace enabled Paul not only to accept his afflictions but even to glory in them. His suffering was not a tyrant that controlled him but a servant that worked for him.

God's sustaining grace enables us to see another purpose. When living with a thorn in the flesh, we need to look beyond the misfortune to see a higher purpose. Perhaps God is using the disappointment to draw our attention to him. We can see only part of the picture, but God sees the entire landscape.

One of the most beautiful Christmas carols we sing is "O Little Town of Bethlehem." Its author, Phillips Brooks, taught in the famous Boston Latin School but failed miserably as a teacher. But through this disappointment he learned that God wanted him to be a preacher, and he became the voice of American Protestantism in the nineteenth century and the author of this great hymn.

God's messages must be read through the envelope in which they are delivered. When we don't get what we want, we need to uncover the true purpose behind it. We need not ask, "Why is this happening to me?" but rather, "What can I learn through this experience?"

Sometimes God says no to us. Sometimes we don't get the Roy Rogers chaps we ask for, or the healing we desire, or the job we want. But in his denial he can still accomplish a great work in and through our lives. The grace that saves us also keeps us. Everything that happens to the child of God is filtered through God's loving hands. Let's not forget that.

Study Questions

1. How did you respond when you did not receive what you wanted?

2. React to the questions "What if God says, 'I've given you my grace, and that is enough'? Will you be satisfied?"

3. How is God a good God when he says no?

4. If you have a thorn in the flesh, why do you think God has not removed it?

5. How has God's grace been sufficient for you?

6. How has God's grace sustained you?

7. How have other people been used as instruments of God's grace to you?

8. How has God's grace enabled you to rise above your tragedies and misfortunes?

Notes

Chapter One: When You Are Running from God
[1]Robert Robinson, "Come, Thou Fount of Every Blessing," in *Baptist Hymnal* (Nashville: Convention Press, 1975), p. 13.
[2]Quoted in *The Oxford Dictionary of Quotations*, 3rd ed. (Oxford: Oxford University Press, 1980), p. 190.
[3]Tony Evans, *Our God Is Awesome* (Chicago: Moody Press, 1994), p. 149.
[4]William R. Newell, "At Calvary," in *Baptist Hymnal*, p. 166.

Chapter Two: When You Need to Change
[1]Quoted in *The Oxford Dictionary of Quotations*, 3rd ed. (Oxford: Oxford University Press, 1980), p. 246.
[2]Quoted in Tim Hansel, *When I Relax I Feel Guilty* (Elgin, Ill.: David C. Cook, 1979), p. 49.

Chapter Three: When You Can't See God
[1]C. Austin Miles, "In the Garden," in *Baptist Hymnal* (Nashville: Convention Press, 1975), p. 428.
[2]Charles Colson, "Making the World Safe for Religion," *Christianity Today*, November 8, 1993, p. 33.
[3]Ida Mae Kemel, "What Was in Jeremy's Egg?" *Focus on the Family*, April 1988, pp. 2-3.

Chapter Four: When You Are Visited by God
[1]Quoted in Elisabeth Elliot, *Shadow of the Almighty* (New York: Harper, 1958), pp. 58-59, 240.

Chapter Five: When You Have to Take a Stand
[1]Steven J. Lawson, *When All Hell Breaks Loose* (Colorado Springs: NavPress, 1993), pp. 45-47.

Chapter Six: When Your Integrity Is Tested
[1]Margie Haack, "Believing Is Seeing," *World*, October 5, 1996, p. 26.
[2]Quoted in *Familiar Quotations*, ed. John Bartlett, 16th ed. (Boston: Little, Brown, 1992), p. 654.
[3]John Maxwell, *Developing the Leader Within You* (Nashville: Thomas Nelson, 1993), p. 39.
[4]Quoted in Robert Andrews, *The Concise Columbia Dictionary of Quotations* (New York: Columbia University Press, 1990), p. 155.
[5]James M. Kouzes and Barry Z. Posner, *The Leadership Challenge* (San Francisco: Jossey-Bass, 1987), p. 16.
[6]Quoted in Charles R. Swindoll, *The Quest for Character* (Portland, Ore.: Multnomah Press, 1987), p. 81.

[7]Quoted in Warren W. Wiersbe, "What Is Integrity?" *Confident Living*, July-August 1988, p. 18.

Chapter Seven: When You Are Treated Unfairly
[1]Quoted in Robert Andrews, *The Concise Columbia Dictionary of Quotations* (New York: Columbia University Press, 1990), p. 289.
[2]Robert S. McGee, *The Search for Significance* (Pasadena, Tex.: Robert S. McGee, 1984), p. 93.
[3]Quoted in *The Treasury of Inspirational Anecdotes, Quotations, and Illustrations*, comp. E. Paul Hovey (Grand Rapids, Mich.: Revell, 1994), p. 137.

Chapter Eight: When You Encounter an Overwhelming Obstacle
[1]Quoted in *The Oxford Dictionary of Quotations*, 3rd ed. (Oxford: Oxford University Press, 1980), p. 132.
[2]Ibid., p. 314.

Chapter Ten: When You Are Hurting
[1]Quoted in *The Treasury of Inspirational Anecdotes, Quotations, and Illustrations*, comp. E. Paul Hovey (Grand Rapids, Mich.: Revell, 1994), p. 204.
[2]Quoted in *The Oxford Dictionary of Quotations*, 3rd ed. (Oxford: Oxford University Press, 1980), p. 572.
[3]Quoted in Hovey, *Treasury of Inspirational Anecdotes*, p. 191.
[4]Quoted in *Oxford Dictionary of Quotations*, p. 578.
[5]Quoted in *Familiar Quotations*, ed. John Bartlett, 16th ed. (Boston: Little, Brown, 1992), p. 362.

Chapter Twelve: When You Don't Get What You Want
[1]Max Lucado, *In the Grip of Grace* (Dallas: Word, 1996), p. 137.